When She Hears The Call

Reconciliation in The Pulpit and The Pew

Jackie L. Green

**The Kuumba House
Communications and Publications
Phoenix, Arizona**

The Kuumba House Communications and Publications is a Christian international organization. Our mission is to help fulfill the Great Commission. (Matthew 28:19-20) through the publishing of creative curriculum, books and creative communications. Kuumba is the Swahili word for "creativity". Our organization encourages the preservation and education of "people of color" to give them a hope for future generations.

The Kuumba House Communications and Publications is the publishing component of Jackie Green Ministries, helping to equip the Body of Christ through preaching, teaching and intercession. Our mission is to equip our readers for the "work of the ministry, and to cover the earth with the Gospel of Jesus Christ."

ISBN: 0-9657931-0-9

Published by The Kuumba House, Communications and Publications, 16845 N. 29th Avenue, Suite 1-138, Phoenix, Arizona 85023-3041 (1 -888-2-Kuumba)

Printed in the United States of America

Front cover. Photo used by permission of Wheelers Photography, Loma Linda, California. Picture of the author and husband (Jackie and Anthony Green).

When She Hears The Call

Reconciliation in The Pulpit and The Pew

Jackie L. Green

Comments from Readers

"*When She Hears The Call* is a well written, fast moving book that I believe will liberate the African American Church. Jackie has a keen understanding into the "wilderness struggles" through which a woman called to ministry must travel. Her book is really helpful for both men and women who have been called to preach as well as those who have family, loved ones and friends who have been called to preach."

Dr. Warren H. Stewart, Sr.
Pastor, First Institutional Baptist Church Phoenix, Arizona and Executive Secretary, Home Mission Board, National Baptist Convention, USA, Inc.

ಜಿ ಜಿ ಜಿ

"I have tremendous affirmation for the book *When She Hears The Call*. I found myself engaged throughout the book as Jackie's deeply personal and moving stories told of how God's call had been made active in her life. The book will be an enriching tool in the lives of women and men in ministry. The story provides practical and poignant help to women pursuing God's call in ministry."

Dr. John Jackson
Former Executive Minister
American Baptist Churches of the Pacific Southwest

"Jackie Green writes with strength and passion concerning a woman's call to preach in her book *When She Hears The Call, Reconciliation in The Pulpit and The Pew*. This is a book that will lift up the women anointed to preach good news. The story will bind up the broken, disillusioned and discouraged who have sought to follow their call and met rejection. This message proclaims truth to those yet captive to their own inhibitions and proclaims the Lord's favor on women who are called to preach."

Dr. Julie Gorman
Associate Professor
Christian Formation & Discipleship
Fuller Theological Seminary, Pasadena, California

ịa ịa ịa

"Having served as Jackie's pastor during her early years, I remember her as one of our young people of whom I was especially proud. In my opinion, *When She Hears The Call* is the most profound and documented material in support of women preachers. Her story deserves the attention of any God called preacher anywhere. In this book she has presented in my opinion, the best support for women preachers I have found anywhere. The most convincing material is the fact that she, individually, answered The Call."

Dr. W. K. Jackson
Pastor Emeritus
St. John Missionary Baptist Church, Oklahoma City, Oklahoma

ịa ịa ịa

"An uncompromising yet non-intimidating challenge to men and women who "hear The Call." Rev. Green set forth this work not only to challenge but to usher in a much needed reconciliation between men and women preachers. She makes clear that though the call is the same, the differences between men and women were never intended to distance the two. This is a must read for every woman who believes "she hears The Call", and every man who seeks to understand and undergird that call."

Dr. James E. Henry
Pastor, Victory Bible Church, Pasadena, California and
Bishop, Western Region Full Gospel Fellowship

🐛 🐛 🐛

"*When She Hears The Call* defines the issues and the struggles in an imminently readable fashion. Rev. Green is faithful to Bible and to Black feminine experience. Her writing indicates a level of care and urgency which might have been dulled within the hearts of others who have "arrived" at her level of proficiency and acceptance. She has recaptured and distilled for a waiting generation of preachers, the very heart wrestlings which many of us lived "just yesterday", but were to encumbered to write about."

Dr. Claudette Anderson Copeland
Pastor, New Creation Christian Fellowship
San Antonio, Texas
(Mentor, D. Min. Program, United Theological Seminary, Dayton, Ohio)

🐛 🐛 🐛

"*When She Hears The Call* is a timely proclamation of facts and truths about women in ministry. The author shares her experiences coupled with conviction to encourage the women of today who have heard The Call, to embrace the *word* with confidence and courage."

Reverend Jean Burch
Founder/Director
Jean Burch Ministries and Women Arise
Los Angeles, California

"I was inspired, sad, thrilled, challenged, committed and convicted. *When She Hears The Call* has opened new thoughts for those of us that still feel it's too late or that we are not as prepared as we feel we should be for The Call. Congregations that are not ready for effective team ministry or how to utilize the expertise of the pastor's wife openly will be challenged."

Doris Carrington, First Lady
Friendship Baptist Church
Yorba Linda, California

&a &a &a

"A life long reference book...*When She Hears The Call* provides compelling spiritual guidance for anyone searching to live the life of God's calling."

Jannah Scott
Layperson
First Institutional Baptist Church
Phoenix, Arizona

Dedication

"For a woman to be a true minister
of Christ these days calls for heroism."
Victoria Booth Demarest

This book is dedicated to all the heroic women
who heard The Call and had the courage
to go forth to preach the Gospel of Jesus Christ.

To all the heroic men that preach
the Gospel of Jesus Christ and have had
the courage to reconcile in God's pulpit
with women preachers.

To my sisters who are yet in THE WILDERNESS....

To my daughter, Elyzabeth.

Table of Contents

Foreword

Today's belated awareness of the harassment of females must include one more atrocity. Women in ministry all too often have to endure being viciously stripped of their self-esteem, robbed of the confidence to trust their hearing of what they know to be the very voice of God. Unlike any other spiritual gift they might have, their vocation of preaching dare not be made public. The pressures of culture and sexism impede even their very inward recognition of The Call. Jackie Green tackles these issues as she describes the experiences of various women drafted by God. She offers wise assistance in dealing with this obligation.

Male-made traditions about women's place in kingdom service; the vigorous opposition of other women; and the continuing demands of parenthood all conspire to thwart the very hearing, to say nothing of answering, the voice of God. Small wonder that any woman manages to survive The Call. How difficult to be obedient to God.

In the pages of this work, the author seeks to help in a variety of ways. She expands the parameters of The Call to include other than the preaching/pastoral ministry, with or without ordination. Women have through the centuries served deeply spiritual functions in the church. With this in mind, the author offers means of coping until the gates to the pulpit are more and more open to women.

The early chapters of this book are devoted to sources of opposition; followed by principles for the implementing of various "rites of passage" into ministerial service. The chapter "Male and Female Midwives to The Call" is a truly unique contribution. This entire work is worthy of serious reading by all Christians, male and female alike.

Dr. Ella Pearson Mitchell
Veteran Theologian
United Theological Seminary
Dayton, Ohio

Preface

When She Hears The Call has finally been birthed. I have carried this baby for eleven years. By the grace of God, I conceived the vision for this book through my trials and tribulations. As the labor pains of birthing my ministry began, God sent spiritual midwives to assist me with each contraction. Jesus promised me He would "never leave me nor forsake me" in the delivery. Somehow it seemed as though what I was birthing was for the sake of "many spiritual" daughters to come.

My prayer is that this book will be a birthing manual for my sisters and even applicable in many instances for the brothers. I believe that when my great-great-granddaughters get a copy of this book, it will still guide them safely to delivery. I believe God has some powerful "preachers in waiting" coming in future generations. I want them to know what I went through but more than that, know the One who will take them through! "For I am confident of this very thing, that He who began a good work in you will perfect it until the day of Christ Jesus." Philippians 1:6

I began thinking about the first time I ever saw or heard a woman preacher. There were none in my sheltered childhood and Baptist upbringing. (I never saw a "woman of the cloth.") I did, however have a deep reverence for "men of the cloth." As a child, my pastor, the Rev. W. K. Jackson of the St. John Baptist Church of Oklahoma City, was the closest thing to God I imagined. When he entered the pulpit in his lavish black velvet robe, all the congregation stood to their feet. I remember always wanting to shake his hand after church. My grandfather was a retired Baptist pastor and I admired his shelves of books, and his quiet encouraging way. Still, I saw no women role models. Women could wear white and be deaconesses, church mothers, missionaries, Sunday school teachers or the best cooks this side of the Jordan. Nothing more, nothing less. By my adult years, I still had not developed a theology about women in ministry. But I found myself defending them just because I felt "the mantle" on their lives deserved respect. I had a fear of the Lord even then, that surely He could choose whom He wanted. The thought never entered my mind that He had chosen me.

While my husband was in seminary in 1973, I met my first woman preacher; her name was Dr. Ella Pearson Mitchell. She and her husband, Dr. Henry H. Mitchell, were resident professors of Colgate Rochester Divinity School. I was just a seminarian's wife. Some years later, I came to realize this was a powerful couple in ministry. Dr. Ella Mitchell is a former visiting Professor of Homiletics at the Interdenominational Theological Center in Atlanta, Georgia and a well-known published theologian with her husband. What a powerful vessel this woman was and what an honor it was to be in her home and just "chat." I believe meeting her was part of my divine destiny. God placed many "markers" in my life to help guide me where I am today.

Another powerful marker was Bishop Leontyne T. C. Kelly, the first African-American woman bishop of a mainline denomination, the United Methodist Church and a visiting Professor of the Pacific School of Religion at Berkeley. I met her in a small group when I went to hear her speak at Fuller Theological Seminary in 1989.

> She said: Be mindful of the people God brings into your life. I hope I disturbed you as the Gospel ought. Never underestimate the changeability of the Gospel for the Spirit moves through individuals...how dare we block it! [1]

Jackie L. Green

Introduction

"Unsent, uncommissioned,
unchosen, uncalled.
'Tis no wonder the land of (Judah) is
in trouble.
There's a profusion of prophets
operating without orders." [2]

I know this book will fall into the hands of pastors, church leaders, and many lay persons who are trying to determine if they have persons in their congregation or even themselves that are sent, commissioned, chosen or called by God to ministry. This book is designed to accomplish three things; (1) help female callees and male callees, respectively, to identify, interpret and implement the call to ministry where preaching is mandated, (2) provide a textbook of pastoral care to assist pastors and congregations with female callees, (3) be a "voice" crying out for reconciliation in God's pulpit to bridge the gap between male and female preachers to function as "one" and bring strength and dignity to the Body of Christ, and help every Christian understand how the call of God works in all our lives.

After my long journey, I can say I know I am called to the ministry with a mandate to preach the Gospel of Jesus

Christ. I have my orders from the Lord. Orders to preach, teach, pioneer new ministries, pray, heal and prophesy. My orders are to set the captives free!

As I look back over my life, beginning at the age of nine, when I received Jesus as my Savior and was baptized, my calling has been a "progressive call." I didn't understand everything about my calling at first.

There are five responses I believe every callee experiences. Three of the responses are internal. The last two responses are external. Some callees experience several of them at once or over a period of time.

At the age of nine, in a very sheltered African-American community in the home of my Baptist grandfather and grandmother, the Christian foundation was being laid. Just like the young boy Samuel, I was raised in an environment conducive of Temple life, but had not yet heard God's voice for myself. At my conversion, I believe The Call was activated. The Word of God declares that from the foundations of the earth, my purpose was already established, even before I was conceived in our mother's womb. (Jeremiah. 1:5 and Ephesians 1:4, 5). My purpose was activated with my confession that Jesus Christ is Lord. Understanding The Call first requires conversion.

This is the first response that every callee must experience. We must first respond to Jesus Christ as our Lord and Savior. No call is activated until there is a conversion experience.

The call to preach is in a category all it's own. And yes, God calls all Christians to the field to serve.

"Every Christian must testify, but
when it comes to The Call to preach,
there must be the agonizing grip of
God's hand on you, your life is in the
grip of God for that one thing." [3]

At age thirteen, in my mother's home in California one
night before going to bed, I sensed The Call. Sensing The
Call through the presence of God is the second response to
understanding one's call. I felt the presence of God enter my
room and "stand" there. I remember asking God "what do
you want with me?" There was no reply, just a "waiting
presence." I knew that I was different from other kids. I
knew I was to be set apart for the Lord. I never told my
mother of this experience. While years passed, I still sensed
that I needed to pursue religious education in college. I had
no other visitation from the Spirit, just a sensing of The Call
that day. One must understand that many things dull our
senses to The Call. Particularly for girls and women, the
fears, traditions, ignorance and even disobedience can de-
lay our understanding of The Call for years. We will look at
these delays in later chapters.

Though I sensed a call at age nine, I was thirty-five years
old before I even allowed myself to be totally compelled.
Twenty-two years later, with sixteen years of marriage, and
three children, in the so-called prime of life, I felt compelled
by The Call. This is the third response in understanding The
Call. I could hear my spirit preaching and see myself in
dreams preaching. I felt like I was going to explode or something. I can remember one Sunday in church feeling so com-

pelled after I had heard the preacher, that I wanted to go up front and tell the whole world, "no longer can I be a secret agent." Instead I shared my calling with my husband in the pastor's study following the service. As my pastor, he asked me to pray about it and he would continue to observe my ministry and pray with me. I enrolled in seminary and began the new journey. The one hundred year old church my husband pastored never had any women ministers, so there were obstacles to be tackled. Two more years past and at age thirty-seven, I answered The Call publicly at a women's conference. The rest is history which I will share in the following pages.

To answer The Call publicly is the fourth response. An external response is required. Callees really struggle with this response because they must now make a public announcement. Some callees stay at this response level for many years.

Finally, the fifth response in understanding The Call is also external and you are sold out to God. You can respond honestly with "God's will, not mine." You are willing to live out your vow in order to fulfill The Call. You are ready to respond by "paying the price" even at the cost of losing your life for the sake of Christ.

To understand The Call, the callee must understand the responses they will go through and that they are not alone in those internal and external responses. Those who have The Call upon their lives can say "been there, done that."

❧ You can answer The Call to the ministry of prayer, helps, writing, hospitality, discipleship, and teaching in some cas-

*es without making a public announcement. But preaching
the Gospel of Jesus Christ requires a public testimony that
must be proclaimed openly and unashamedly.*

I want to define some of the terms I will be referring to throughout the book. I realized after talking with many female and male callees that there were many different experiences, expectations and definitions for terms like preacher, call to ministry, call to preach, callee, and midwife. I want to take time to explain the context in which I will be using these terms.

1. Call to ministry- when a person by a divine experience with God feels a responsibility (burden) to serve God by dedicating his or her life in a field of Christian service, not necessarily with a mandate to preach. There are many fields of Christian service that do not require one to serve by preaching. There are social, educational, recreational, medical, psychological, economical and many other arenas to serve this present age.

2. The Call - is a call to ministry with a responsibility (mandate) to preach the Gospel of Jesus Christ along with other ministerial functions.

3. Callee - a layperson (male or female or child) who has recognized and accepted God's call upon their lives to a call to ministry that mandates preaching.

4. Preacher - a preacher is merely "a voice" used by God that can be male, female or child to proclaim, practice and press. To preach is to proclaim or declare the Gospel of Jesus Christ. A preacher then is a herald or one that announces the Good News. When we use this term

"preacher" it is more than one that stands in a pulpit with oratorical ability and charisma. To be a preacher means to; (1) proclaim the Gospel of Jesus Christ (vocal), (2) to practice with one's whole life what one preaches, and (3) to press toward the fulfillment of that call with preparation and service through excellence.

5. Midwife - a person (male or female) whom God uses to help the callee mature educationally, experientially and ecclesiastically in order to fulfill their call to ministry. Usually a midwife is the local pastor, congregation, family members in many cases, the Christian community-at-large and personal mentors.

6. Clergy - Men and women set apart by ordination for the service of God as religious leaders; persons who vocationally are recognized by the Body of Christ and the community as a professional trained in their field of ministry.

Historically in the African-American Church the phrase The Call applied to the readiness to preach the Gospel. Saints can feel a calling to many areas of ministry in the church, but the preaching ministry must be acknowledged by experiencing The Call from God Himself. The Call has with it a mysteriousness, a personal experience, a sense of called-outness, an anointing all its own. There was a time when I was growing up, The Call, in the African-American tradition, was the highest position of dedication in one's life to God.

When I meet preachers that treat the Gospel like an elective choice or alternative, I am disturbed. Preaching must be passion not a pastime. Preaching shouldn't supplement our income; be a way to pick up extra money, or pacify God just enough for our good conscience. We must be willing to give up all, adjust all, rearrange all, and prioritize all for The Call.

> The Call is a rites of passage ritual whereby a lay person moves through a threshold to become a member of clergy. [4]

⅋ The Call must be accepted as a divine mandate, not an elective.

What we learn from 1 Samuel, 3 through the calling of the boy Samuel to the prophetic office are some powerful principles to help every callee, male and female alike. The Hebrew word "call" in this scripture is "qara" meaning to be subpoenaed or drafted for service.

Principle #1 - The Call is divine (supernatural) but still must be heard through our human environment.

1 Samuel 3:4-10, 15, 18

4   *That the Lord called Samuel; and he said, "Here am I."*

5   *Then he ran to Eli and said, "Here am I, for you called me." But he said, "I did not call, lie down again", so he went and lay down.*

6   *And the Lord called yet again, "Samuel!" So Samuel arose and went to Eli, and said, "Here I am, for you called me." But he answered, "I did not call, my son, lie down again."*

7   *Now Samuel did not yet know the Lord, nor had the word of the Lord yet been revealed to him.*

8   *So the Lord called Samuel again for the third time. And he arose and went to Eli, and said, "Here I am, for you called me." Then Eli discerned that the Lord was calling the boy.*

9   *And Eli said to Samuel, "Go lie down, and it shall be if He calls you, that you shall say Speak, Lord, for thy servant is listening." So Samuel went and lay down in his place.*

10   *Then the Lord came and stood and called as at the other times, "Samuel, Samuel!" and Samuel said, "Speak, for thy servant is listening."*

15   *So Samuel lay down until morning. Then he opened the doors of the house of the Lord. But Samuel was afraid to tell the vision to Eli.*

18   *So Samuel told him everything and hid nothing from him. And he said, "It is the Lord. Let Him do what seems good to Him."*

1 Samuel 3 makes it clear that little Samuel in his humanness, in the temple, a sheltered environment, does hear a voice. But in Samuel's naiveté and since God's voice was rare in those days, he did not recognize the voice of the Lord. Samuel had no idea what God's voice sounded like. He mistakes God's voice for Eli's voice. What other person could be calling for him especially at this hour? But God still had to find a way to speak to Samuel in his human environment. God used a "seasoned preacher" to help interpret His voice. We don't always hear God's call because we are unfamiliar with Him. Hearing impairments such as our unfamiliarity, humanness, carnality, sin and outright

disobedience play a major role in our spiritual hearing. Hearing God requires being able to properly identify His voice.

Bishop Leontine T. C. Kelly gives a powerful testimony on The Call as the first woman Bishop, an African-American woman to head the United Methodist denomination.

> I believe in a called ministry, a sense of assurance that there is something specific for you to do...Paul didn't call me. I believe God called me to the ordained ministry. I was willing to go that journey and it has been sustained. [5]

Principle #2 - The Call is not returnable to the sender.

1 Samuel 3: 4-10 describes a very interesting side of God that we overlook. God will not be ignored. He will call us as many times as necessary to get us to hear and respond. God called little Samuel three times and the fourth time God got a response. Who can ignore God? God recognizes the interferences we encounter with hearing spiritually. So, He patiently waits and stands by until we get the right frequency. God will summons until we hear and respond.

In 1905, Preacher E. J. Sheeks gives her response to The Call:

> In my prayers this call was before me, and as I would listen to others preach, I would really tremble as I felt it was only a question of time when I would have to do the same

thing or lose my soul. I was very con-
scious of my inability, so I offered
many excuses to the Lord. But he
continued to press The Call upon me.
I knew to accept The Call to preach
meant sacrifice, self-denial, reproach,
opposition and persecution. [6]

The Bible says that a thousand years is as a day. God will
not run out of time. For some, God has been subpoenaing
them for years. He's not tired or weary. The gifts and calling
of God are irreversible. God knew that Samuel would even-
tually hear and respond. God has all the time in the world
and eternity. But we must be mindful we are limited in our
time to respond to The Call.

*Once we hear right, we can respond right. And once we
respond right, we can live right.*

Another important component of
The Call experience is signs. Signs include voices, visions, and other concomitant events. As the following
discussion will reveal, "voices" refers
to the perception of divine communi-
cation, and "vision" is used as a syn-
onym for dream or trance. Other
concomitant events are varied in nature, including such phenomena as
car accidents, bright lights from the
sky, and hospital operations. [7]

Samuel did not hear right at first. He thought Eli was

calling him. God so graciously touched Eli's discernment and Eli helped Samuel hear right. God has "hearing aids" for us all. For Samuel it was his long and trusted teacher, Eli. For you and I it could be someone near by or most assuredly, the Holy Spirit to help us hear. Some of us may need events and divine encounters to help us hear effectively.

Three hearing aides that are most helpful to us are the Word of God, The Holy Spirit and a life of prayer. The Word of God is a hearing aide; by the Word we hear and our faith comes. The Holy Spirit the (Paraclete) is also a great hearing aide sent for the purpose to help us hear and see. The callee must have "a prayer life" if they are going to be able to hear from the Lord.

Aimee Semple McPherson, early woman Evangelist and founder of the Foursquare Gospel Churches describes her call to preach on her death bed:

> The voice had kept on, she still resist-
> ing, until one night, about two
> o'clock in the morning, she heard a
> nurse murmur, "she's going", and
> everything went black. Then in her
> words before losing consciousness
> came the voice of the Lord..."now
> will you go?"
> "Yes Lord, I'll go." [8]

❧ *The Call follows us even to the grave. If you don't answer on earth, you will give an account when you stand before the Lord.*

The late Barbara Ann Wilson, founder of Clergy Women

United, Los Angeles (Barbara Ann Wilson Chapter) shares her testimony on videotape before her death. Her Jonah experience makes it clear that The Call is serious with God. Barbara was a licensed social worker and counselor. She decided after many years of her profession to retire and open a flower shop. While in the flower shop, face down, her heart having arrested, The Call again was put before her. She promised God she would preach. After coming out of intensive care, she again resisted The Call. She had a second incident with her heart having arrested and God's voice getting stronger. This time she decided no matter what anyone said, she would obey God. Barbara was one of the pioneer women (in her mid-thirties) to pursue her calling, began seminary, organized a Clergy Women United chapter in Los Angeles and was called home to glory a year later. She made a tremendous impact on the lives of women in ministry in her short time of obedience. The scholarship developed in her name at Fuller Theological Seminary assisted me with over four thousand dollars in scholarship funds. I never met her, but I owe much to her obedience to The Call.

Because of Reverend Barbara Ann Wilson's life, she helped me and many other middle aged women deal with what I call "a late start." I have talked with many women preachers who came into the fullness of their call in much later years due to delayed responses and stumbling blocks. They feel that they have wasted a lot of time and minister now under a cloud of condemnation.

In my own licensing service as I preached my trial sermon, I was moved to close my sermon with my own testimony of how I had waited so long to respond to God in The Call. But God spoke to my heart and let me know He is not limited by a time clock. He can redeem time, extend time, make time stand still or make time abound on our behalf. He told me to "Go ahead and preach. Don't go in fear, just go in my Name." And so to my sisters and brothers who feel they have had a "late start", God is able to allow you to fulfill your vow to Him right where you are.

Principle #3 - The Call is no respecter of persons. God is only looking for a voice, not a gender.

Samuel had not developed in the area of the spirit world and thusly his discernment had not been developed yet. He had no comprehension that God, the creator of the world would speak into his little world. Samuel's eyes had not been opened to the character and ways of God. God's way was to speak and call a young lad to do His bidding. Surely Eli should be the one that God speaks to. No. It was an unsuspecting, young, tender, pure servant boy that God would call.

ﾏ **God calls from the inside out, for He looks on the heart and not the outer appearance.**

Samuel knew God for what he had learned externally but now God would call him "internally." Samuel would now begin to know (Hebrew: yada) God intimately, sense and perceive Him and discern God from within. This is the way God calls. With this principle, we can clear up the myths that God would not call a woman, or how can we prove that anyone has really been called?

Ever since the apostles prayed and

cast lots to find a replacement for Judas, the church has wrestled with the call to ministry and how it is recognized, affirmed, or denied. Times have changed, along with church policy, but the idea of calling continues to be a gender-related controversy today. [9]

Though the controversy continues today, God is no respecter of persons. The Bible has recorded God calling male and females, Jews and Gentiles and even young children.

To fight the Spirit of God in a woman is to fight God himself. God is not divided against Himself. The Spirit of God in a male minister would not fight the Spirit of God in a female minister. The spirit of envy perhaps. The spirit of pride. The spirit of competition. But never the Spirit of God. [10]

Further, Jeremiah describes His call as "fire, shut up in his bones." You could not see this fire inside Jeremiah, but The Call of God always begins inside and proceeds outward.

The late Kathryn Kuhlman, worldwide Evangelist, expressed her call from the "inside that proceeded outward" in the following way: Kathryn unable to control her weeping, put her head in Myrtle's lap and sobbed for long minutes.

"All those people who didn't receive
Jesus as their Savior. Didn't you feel
it too?"
"Feel what Kathryn?"
"Feel the burden for the lost. I must
preach. I'll never be satisfied until I
am doing my share."
She felt she was under divine mandate. [11]

**Principle #4 - Inevitably, we must hear The Call for our-
selves in order to be sent.**

1 Samuel 3: 9-10 describes this principle. Though Eli assisted little Samuel in listening for the Lord's voice, Samuel
still had to hear The Call for himself. This is pivotal.

Many are posing and passing as real.[12] One should be convincingly con-
scious of a divine call. Furthermore,
he should have a gospel to preach,
and he must be empowered to preach
it. [13]

While attending Fuller Theological Seminary, I was dis-
tressed to meet so many seminarians still not sure of The
Call. Because of the African-American tradition of establish-
ing The Call first, you did not go to school or practice on
people to bring assurance. Many students (probably due to
their traditions) were working on a second master's degree,
or in a parish, and still had no real conviction to The Call.
Many of them were pastoring, preaching, doing a religious
vocation but not because of assurance of The Call. For many

it was a good field or vocation to be in.

> When God wishes His Word to be
> proclaimed, this does not exclude the
> possibility that a person doing the
> proclaiming genuinely wants to do it.
> A preacher would be crippled with-
> out a consciousness of being called.
> One of the most terrible agonies a
> preacher can experience is becoming
> inwardly unsure about whether to
> preach or not. [14]

An elderly gentleman from our church, by the name of
Deacon Floyd Fortson of Second Baptist Church of Redlands, California, used to say, "Were you sent or did you
just went?"

> You've got to be called and chosen.
> You've got to be appointed and
> anointed. What an error the church
> makes when she plays down the idea
> of a "divine calling" to preach the
> Gospel. What a violence we do the
> souls of people when we put preach-
> ing in the same category as other pro-
> fessions. What a mockery we make of
> the ministry when we recruit for
> seminaries without The Call being
> primary criteria. [15]

Principle #5 - The Call will show some signs.

The principle from this text can be found in 1 Samuel 3:

15-18. As soon as The Call was received by Samuel, there was evidence of The Call. Samuel now has foreknowledge he did not have before regarding his mentor Eli and his sons. Samuel begins to manifest the mind and purposes of God regarding Eli's future. The prophetic anointing is at work. Eli prompts the child and commands Samuel to tell him all that the Lord had revealed to him. Eli knew from the words of the child that The Call was there. The Call could not be questioned for it witnessed of the Lord. Eli responds by saying, "...It is the Lord." The Call will always point back to the Lord and give glory to God. The Call will be confirmed by others. I shall never forget before I was licensed to preach, The Call was evident in my life. God was sending me out to minister while our church was discussing "what shall we do with her?" I was scheduled to preach at a large church in Los Angeles. The newspaper article announced... "Rev. Jackie Green to speak at St. Paul Baptist Church of Los Angeles." Dr. Lefall, the pastor, greeted me warmly. He was aware in a previous phone call of my church's struggle with licensing women called to preach. When he saw me, he said, "You're a preacher. Come with me to the pulpit." In other words, there must have been something about my demeanor and message that confirmed "it is the Lord" in her life. The Spirit confirmed The Call even before "men" could decide the procedure. The Call will have evidence and signs following. It's as though God "marks" His preachers. Others just know. The presence of God will be on your life. We must walk as one whom the Spirit of the Lord is upon. Then once you open your mouth, as with young Samuel, it will be further evident that you are called.

Dr. Ella Mitchell describes signs from her early years of ministry. It was after she had preached that signs followed indicating God was "with her."

> I shall never forget how on another Sunday in a remodeled garage in a California city, eleven souls came forward to surrender their lives to Christ. This time nine of them were candidates for baptism. The pastor, God bless him, with tears in his eyes proclaimed things about my ministry that up to that time I had not the nerve even to think for myself. God moves in mysterious and unrestricted ways. [16]

In summarizing this chapter, I think the words of Dr. D. E. King's book, *Preaching to Preachers* captures the importance of a divine call.

> Before you stand to preach, first present your moving identification conviction as proof of a divine call. Without this, even if you stand up, you will not be a Gospel preacher. If God means for you to preach, He will tell you so, personally. He will not leave you guessing. He will strive with you until you cannot keep from preaching. [17]

These five principles that we glean from The Call of young Samuel are meant to help the callee identify a divine call on their life. In summary, The Call must be divinely inspired, The Call is not returnable to sender: thirdly, The Call is no respecter of persons: fourthly, The Call must be heard by the callee themselves and lastly, The Call will show some signs.

Now that we have identified The Call through internal and external responses, and laid a foundation for the biblical understanding of how to identify The Call, we shall now focus on helping callees interpret The Call. Chapters 1 through 3 will discuss how the *stumbling blocks, assurances and wilderness experiences affect how we identify* The Call. Chapters 4 through 6 will help the callee interpret issues and the reality of The Call. And finally, Chapters 7 through 9 will provide pastoral care for the callee to implement their call.

Jackie L Green

Chapter 1
Seven Stumbling Blocks
to The Call

🍃 *It's time we learn how to turn our stumbling blocks into stepping stones which is evidence of a genuine call.*

As I prayed about this section, I asked the Holy Spirit to reveal the areas that have been major stumbling blocks for women callees and the Body of Christ. As I read books written by women preachers as far back as the 1800s, I discovered the exact same stumbling blocks still exist today. There has been progress but some major strongholds still exist. We must turn these stumbling blocks into stepping stones. There has been a stronghold of deception concerning God's calling of women to the pulpit. The only way to rise above the stumbling block of deception is to rightly divide the word of truth. That brings us to our first major stumbling block.

Stumbling Block #1 - Restricted Interpretation of Scriptures Related to Women

This stumbling block is a historical stronghold. What has historically been taught is often hard to change. We know that history books are usually written by the dominant people group, or ruling power structures. So it is with Scripture interpretation in our churches regarding women in the church. Men have been the writers, men have been the leaders and in most cases men have been the major oppressors of women in the church life. We see this historical view coming down through the Old Testament treatment of women in Jewish traditions. We will further see how the mindset of the adversary has caused women even to hate themselves or doubt that God could call them for anything.

Two key Scriptures come to mind which establish the plan of God to use both male and females to preach the Gospel. Joel 2:28-29 and Acts 2:17-18 gives us validation in the Old Testament and New Testament for a balanced, equal opportunity service to God.

> *And it will come about after this that I will pour out My spirit on all mankind; and your sons and daughters will prophesy, your old men will dream dreams, your young men will see visions. And even on the male and female servants I will pour out My Spirit in those days. Joel 2:28-29 And it shall be in the last days,' God says, 'that I will pour forth of My Spirit upon all mankind, and your sons and your daughters shall prophesy, and your young men shall see visions, and your old men shall dream dreams; even upon My bondslaves, both men and women, I will in those days pour forth of My Spirit and they shall prophesy. Acts 2:17-18*

I find that those who have kept the "GREAT DISPUTE" (women preachers) going through the years ignore this passage of scripture or debate the real meaning of "prophesy" in both Joel and Acts.

Joel 2:28 and Acts 2:17-18 has been challenged by some to mean that "prophesy" in these text is not validation for the same word as preaching. Therefore, some feel that this text is not strong enough to validate women having the spirit poured out on them to "preach." This is a good point and with further research we find that the Old Testament meaning of "prophesy or prophet's role" is somewhat different and expanded in the New Testament.

The Expository Dictionary of New Testament Words clarifies the role of the Old Testament and New Testament role of the prophet:

> In the case of the Old Testament prophets, their messages were largely the proclamation of the Divine purposes of salvation and glory to be accomplished in the future; the prophesying of the New Testament prophets was both a preaching of the Divine counsels of grace already accomplished and the fore-telling of the purposes of God in the future. [18]

To further get an understanding of the New Testament role of prophesy we can look at the life of our Lord Jesus Christ, (the prophet of Nazareth of Galilee) functioning as a New Testament prophet Himself. His functions included:

...fulfillment of that which was already prophesied

...preaching

...teaching, healing, and miracles

...declaring the Word of God

...prayer

...casting out demons

...stills the storms

...calling and ordaining of apostles/disciples

...speaking forth mysteries and parables

...foretelling of future events (His own death, burial, resurrection)

...ministry to multitudes

...ministry with great authority and power

This is a clear view on how the New Testament prophet would function. Different from the Old Testament, the New Testament prophet would be called a preacher instead of "seer."

The following chart can help us in understanding what it means for our "sons and daughters" that prophesy. We can compare the signs that followed the Old Testament person that prophesied to the New Testament person that would prophesy.

Old Testament Signs/Titles/Tasks Describing the Prophetic Ministry	New Testament Signs/Titles/Tasks Describing the Prophetic Ministry
Speak forth by divine utterance	Speak forth by divine utterance
Pastor, Shepherd of the people, Seer	Preacher, Pastor
Miracles/healings	Miracles/healings
Watchmen on the wall/Intercessors	Intercessory ministry
Teachers of the law	Teacher and maker of disciples
Dreams and visions	Dreams and visions
Spoke of Israel's future	Speak of the end times/Second Coming/Kingdom of God/Heaven
Reprove/pronounce judgment on the people for sins	Preach repentance/forgiveness of sins/Salvation by blood of Jesus Christ

We need to understand the words of Dr. Warren H. Stewart, Sr., Pastor of the First Institutional Baptist Church of Phoenix, Arizona, (when he preached at my ordination):

> Some of you are wondering why so many women are going into the ministry. You need to check your watches and see what time it is! You better check with the Holy Ghost and see what time it is!...we are living in the fullness of time! [19]

We have stumbled over the word "prophesy" and over restricted interpretations of this text. We have ignored the "anointing" that is apparent on women callees and held fast to limited revelations.

In other words, THIS IS THAT which the Prophet Joel prophesied. The Lord laid on my heart that the church has either misinterpreted Scripture, malpracticed Scripture or simply torn certain sections out of the Bible all together! We cannot ignore Joel's prophecy! We are experiencing the prophecy now! Restricted interpretation will not stop the libation of God's Spirit on all flesh! Joel tells of God pouring out His Spirit on all flesh, male and female, old men and young men, and all flesh I believe includes "children."

Joel 2:28-29 and Acts 2:18-18 are generally ignored while 1 Corinthians 14:34-35 and 1 Timothy 2:12 are used as the "bashing" Scriptures. 1 Corinthians 14:34-35 is most familiar:

> *Let your women(wives) keep silent in the churches; for they are not permitted to speak, but let them subject them-*

selves, just as the law also says. And if they desire to learn anything, let them ask their own husbands at home; for it is improper for a woman (wife) to speak in church.

1 Timothy 2:12 reads:

But I do not allow a woman (wife) to teach or exercise authority over a man (husband), but to remain quiet.

Once you study the text, and keep the text in context of what Paul is teaching the church at Corinth, the following needs to be clarified:

1. Paul is speaking in 1 Corinthians 14 to women (wives) (Greek-*gune*) to ask their own husbands questions at home and not to disrupt his teaching time. We know that Paul already permitted the women to pray and prophesy (preach) in 1 Corinthians. 11:5. Paul here is not speaking about women being silent when it comes to their preaching. He is talking to married women, and not preaching women.

This text is dealing with relationships between a husband and wife in the church. Wives were not to override their husbands in spiritual matters, especially in church.

❧ *I am amazed how male pastors have used this Scripture against women. It was never taught as a Scripture for husbands and wives. But they don't tell women to be silent in the church when they are raising money for the church, selling chicken dinners, teaching Sunday school or speaking to build up their own ministries.*

There has been great abuse of this text. Remember also that the early churches were many times "house churches." That meant that many couples may have hosted the church services in their homes, thusly it became important how husbands and wives conducted themselves in the assembly of believers. Paul addresses this issue that must have been getting out of hand between husbands and wives. This text has nothing to do with whether or not a woman can preach the Gospel. The text is a domestic issue.

2. Paul, in 1 Timothy 2:12, explains that women (wives) are not to usurp authority over a man (husband). I agree. However, if God has called a woman to preach and has anointed her in a particular office to teach, pastor, prophesy, then she is not usurping authority. *Usurping authority is using authority that has not been given to you by God.* But, for that matter, neither does God allow men to usurp authority where it is not given to them. (Example, where a deacon or trustee usurps authority over the pastor.) This happens more than we want to acknowledge.

These two Scriptures have been used to "batter" women in ministry and cause division in the Body of Christ. God is not pleased. We must rightly divide the word of truth.

> The Queens of different countries exercise authority over men, but no one considers them as usurpers. [20]

Why did Paul address the issue of women and the use of authority in the church? Paul would be grieved today to know that hundreds of years later, we took his Epistles and used them as a weapons against each other. A missionary gives us a sensible reason why Paul makes the statement in 1 Corinthians 14:34-35:

> Missionaries tell us that the same an-

noying custom prevails in the Oriental lands today. The Rev. R L. Harris (deceased), said that he never knew the meaning of 1 Corinthians 14:34 until he went as a missionary to Africa. He said that the women are kept in ignorance, but that the men are educated. He also said it was considered a disgrace for a girl when she reaches womanhood not to get married. As soon as they are grown, they enter into a marriage relation. When he began to conduct religious services, many of them would attend with their husbands. They were so very ignorant they could not comprehend even his plain preaching of the Gospel. So they would interrupt him by asking questions while he was giving the Gospel message. [21]

🐦 *Thank God He is raising up a militant church in these last days and a studying church. The Body of Christ will no longer accept watered down truth. The stronghold of restricted interpretation and historical strongholds in Scripture will be broken by applying the whole truth of God's Word, and reteaching the Scriptures.*

In dealing with the stumbling block of restricted interpretation of Scripture, it is important that pastors, churches and denominations repent and begin to teach the whole counsel of God. If they feel they cannot, then Acts 5:38-39 says it well and I want to paraphrase it:

And now I say unto you, refrain from these (women preachers), and let them alone; for if this counsel or this work be of (women alone), it will come to naught. But if it be of God, ye cannot overthrow (them). Lest ye be found even to fight against God.

In essence, we need to hear what the Spirit is saying to the church on this issue. Pastors, congregations and whole denominations need to be sure that what they are teaching:

1. Brings glory to God;
2. Is consistent with the life and ministry of Jesus' treatment toward women;
3. Witnesses with the Holy Spirit and how He is moving today in the Body of Christ.

Stumbling Block #2 - Rejection by Male Ministers, Congregations, Denominations and Other Women

To reject what we fear or do not understand is human nature. However, the Body of Christ is not called to operate by human nature, but by the leading of the Holy Spirit.

> *He is despised and forsaken of men, a man of sorrows and acquainted with grief; and like from whom men hid their face, He was despised and we did not esteem Him. Isaiah 53:3*
>
> *But Jesus said to them, "You do not know what you are asking for. Are you able to drink of the cup that I drink of? Or to be baptized with the baptism with which I am baptized?" Mark 10:38*

❧ *Many women preachers had horrible memories of inci-*

dents related to their call or another woman's experience.
Jesus has provided for us through His blood the healing for
rejection.

Rejection is defined by *Webster's Dictionary* as refusing
to accept someone, or recognize or make use of; to deny or
discard as useless or to spit out or vomit.

Rejection is a major stumbling block for male and female
callees.

> Some men state they encountered re-
> sistance from family, friends, pastors
> and others. However, this usually
> deals with economics, expectations,
> age, or some other factor, never gen-
> der. [22]

Rejection for the female callee is much deeper. Whole
denominations justify widespread rejection of women
callees throughout the Body of Christ. Again, I remind us
that this is not a small sore in the Body of Christ. It is a widespread cancer. Many women callees expect rejection auto-
matically depending on her background and orientation.
Men callees don't have the depth of rejection to deal with as
women. Rejection from our support systems (family, pastor,
church, religious community) can be a real hindrance to any
callee. Refer to the Callee Journey Chart in Chapter 2 to see
how rejection from the support systems make the callee
journey to ministry fulfillment very difficult.

The Scripture in Isaiah 53:3 is a reminder that our Lord
faced rejection for different reasons, but it was rejection just
the same. We learn from our Lord's life and example, that

ministry can bring some rejection from the world and even the church itself. We must never let rejection stop us from accomplishing God's purpose and call for our lives.

David Seamands recommends something he calls "divine repair" for damaged emotions, and six biblical steps to receive healing:

What is our part in the healing of damaged emotions? The Holy Spirit is, indeed, the divine counselor, the divine psychiatrist, who gets a hold of our problem on the other end. But we're on this end of it. We must (1) face the problem squarely, (2) accept responsibility in the matter, (3) ask yourself if you want to be healed, (4) forgive everyone who is involved in your problem, (5) forgive yourself and, (6) ask the Holy Spirit to show you what your real problem is, and how you need to pray.[23]

While meeting with two sister clergy for a time of prayer and sharing, one sister began to share about memories of the past hurts where she saw women in ministry "made fun of" and not taken seriously. This had become a stumbling block to her even accepting the fact that God would call her to pastor one day. It was in this meeting that God spoke to us that our stumbling blocks can be transformed into stepping stones.

We can learn from our Lord Jesus Christ how He kept focused on what His Father sent Him to earth to do. We will never experience the fullness of the rejection that Jesus felt. Yet, in His humanness He dealt with rejection. He suffered rejection for our sake.

🍂 *Jesus overcame every form of rejection at the Cross.*

There is open rejection, there is silent rejection, and there is even rejection in the womb before birth.

The greatest rejection that I experienced is the silent rejection from the pew. You are ignored. You are tolerated but there is really no provision for your ministry. In certain churches you are never called to the pulpit or acknowledged. I have even had women stare with a "rejection stare" or "evil eye" that says, "who does she think she is?" Yes, even in the church you can get stared down. The spirit of rejection has many motivations but only one root, FEAR. But there is a balm, a healing agent for the wounded spirit.

John and Paula Sanford in their book Healing The Wounded Spirit conclude that:

> We have stated that Jesus is able to transcend time and identify with us at any stage of our development, to set us free from those dated emotions and expectations which shape the basic structure of our being and hold us in bondage. [24]

> At night shepherds felt the faces and ears of sheep for ticks. Finding some, they did not pluck them for fear of

leaving a portion which could cause
disease. Instead, they poured on oil
until suffocating ticks were forced to
back out. But the oil accomplished
more than that. It soothed dry, sun
parched skin. It entered the wound
and acted as an antiseptic balm. But
most importantly, it simply comfort-
ed and healed. [25]

Our Shepherd does the same for us today who have
been wounded and scarred. The oil of the Spirit suffocates
rejections, bad experiences and emotional scars and soothes
us. The blood of Jesus washes away any power of rejection.
The Great Shepherd knows how to comfort us. He is the
bondage breaker. We must minister inspite of our limp. We
must obey God in the face of rejection.

I want to share a very unique story that happened to me;
a story that gave me insight as to how God sees us as wom-
en who have been rejected for His sake. While I was in Los
Angeles at a international prayer conference, I spent two
days in the intercessory prayer room. I met intercessors
from all over the United States. There was a male intercessor
whom I had met during the time of prayer. He and his wife
were called to prayer. As I prepared to leave the room to go
back to Arizona, he came outside and stopped me. He
looked at me and said God had shown him that "I was one
of them." I said to him "What do you mean?" He said he
sensed that I was one of the many women in the Body of
Christ that had weathered rejection for preaching the Gos-

pel. He shared a vision God gave him concerning the rejection of women in ministry. He saw God sitting on the throne in heaven. Periodically it seemed that three or four women in white, with their faces covered, would come to the throne and bow before the Lord. As they left the throne, he saw their scared and disfigured faces. He then asked God, "What happened to them?" God replied, "They are my handmaidens that I called to carry my Gospel. The have been rejected, maimed and wounded for my sake. The scars are from pastors, churches and Christians mostly in my Body that have rejected and hurt them. But they continue to 'bring in the harvest of souls' to me."

This story always brings me great strength for I am "one of them" that has been scarred for the sake of Christ, but I vowed to continue to bring in the harvest to my Lord! Hallelujah! I may be rejected, but I have a reward coming from the Lord!

❧ *You know you are "called" when you can preach inspite of your wounds; you know you are healed when your wounds become your trophy.*

There are three things I want to say to wounded callees who have experienced rejection:

1. Some rejection comes with The Call anyway. Rejection is in the cup as we share in the sufferings of Jesus Christ. You'll have to preach even when others reject you. But never let their rejection of your God given qualities impede you. Remember who you are and whose you are.

2. Our Lord Jesus Christ is master in overcoming rejection. He kept His eyes on the Father and was always about

the Father's business. There is no rejection He can't heal.
Jesus is Lord over rejection. Rejection must bow its knee
to Jesus as you obey Him. Keep your eyes on Jesus.
While you obey, He fights your battles.

3. Jesus has called us to be an example. He will use the
lowly and humble, male or female, and exalt them in
due time. Don't let rejection rule you or make you bitter.

A word of caution was given to me at my ordination by
Dr. James Henry, Pastor of Victory Bible Church of Pasadena, California.

> I charge you never spend a day defending your call. And never spend a day damning those men who don't receive it. I charge you to go wherever He sends you and never look at their faces but be consumed with His face. I charge you to pray more than you preach. For the power in your preaching comes from the power of your praying. Pray more than you preach. [26]

Though his charge cautioned me against rejection by
men, I would say that his advice applies to rejection from
women as well.

The Rev. Fannie E. Suddarth describes the informed
prejudice against women preachers as coming from her
own mother.

> I must confess to an inborn prejudice against all attempts on the part of any

woman to be heard speaking or praying in a public congregation. My pru-
dent and decorous mother had given
me timely lectures on the gross im-
propriety of violating Paul's com-
mand: "Let your women keep silent
in the churches." [27]

&❧ *Our mothers and grandmothers passed down to us an
oppressive heritage. They too had been oppressed. But now
we must make sure our sons and daughters inherit all the
promises and not allow history to repeat itself.*

Stumbling Block #3 - Traditions of Men

*...thus invalidating the Word of God by your tradition
which you have handed down, and you do many things
such as that. Mark 7:13*

I can only speak from an African-American Baptist per-
spective on the treatment of women called to preach the
Gospel. Yet, there are now many Baptist churches acknowl-
edging that God can use women in the ministry. We have
not been as progressive as other denominations.

While attending a national convention of Baptists in
Oklahoma City several years ago, it was evident that
something was missing. There were thousands of delegates
there, but I was yet a "secret agent," preacher. There was no
one there to affirm women in the ministry on the platform.
If you attended the convention, you had an understanding
that "there would be none of that here." Women have been
accepted in the African-American Baptist tradition as
Evangelists. Women were still treated with a long-handled

spoon and not as equals. As I looked on the podium at the convention, there were no women preachers. What a tragedy! In the words of Dr. David DuPlessis, the father of the Pentecostal Movement, he asked:

> "Where are the women pastors?" The moderator replied: "There are no women here, just men pastors." Dr. DuPlessis then said, "I won't be here either, speaking to half a man." [28]

In essence, he recognized that the body was not complete without both male and female representation of Christ. I felt a great stagnation, a great grieving because after more than one hundred years, many Christians are still operating under the stronghold of tradition concerning women female clergy. This is a tradition that has been handed down to us-it is a spiritual stronghold that we must break. I believe the cloud of the Spirit is moving and many conventions/denominations need to get under the cloud once again.

❧ *When traditions interfere with what God is doing, He will raise up a new movement. Whereas God would desire to use the local church to usher in His Spirit, He has chosen to utilize national conferences and retreats to accomplish His purpose and bless the Body of Christ inspite of themselves.*

In closing on tradition, my family is Baptist born and Baptist bred! I did not know how my family would respond to my call. I had made a decision however, that I loved them but I loved Jesus more. I was prepared for rejection and even excommunication. But that didn't happen. My parents and most of my relatives received me and have supported me in my life decision to preach the Gospel.

I need to say here that the "traditional spirit" is closely tied to the "religious spirit," both invalidate the Word of God (Mark 7:13) by the traditions we have handed down. Jesus teaches us several things about dealing with tradition or the religious spirit of the Pharisees: The religious spirit is a spirit that has a form of godliness but denies the power thereof. (2 Timothy 3:5). Their religion is only in their creeds but not their hearts.

Their hearts are like cement; cold, rigid and sometimes evil.

You will know a religious spirit is operating in a church when people prefer to keep things the way they've always been instead of allowing the Holy Spirit to set people free or do something out of the ordinary.

Jesus did not judge them because they were so rigid in traditions and the law. He taught, preached and healed those that were ready to hear. God has an audience for you. Don't worry if your church does not receive you because of tradition. God sent me out to preach more than I was preaching in house. This kept me from being judgmental and in strife with the people. Those times of preaching kept me alive! Stay put if God does not move you. We must be willing to pioneer new things, and that's not always easy.

Stumbling Block #4 - The Battle with Satan

Ignorance of spiritual warfare has caused us to stumble. *And I will put enmity between thee and the woman, and*

between thy seed and her seed; it shall bruise thy head, an
thou shalt bruise his heel. Genesis 3:15
❧ *I believe women preachers have more fiery darts thrown*
at them because of the enmity that originated in the garden.
The war on women began in the garden.

This is also the one key reason that it has taken so long
for women to come forth in the ministry and be co-laborers
with men. Women preachers pose a double threat to the
kingdom of darkness. Firstly, they can birth children into
the earth realm that are potential souls for the Kingdom of
God. Secondly, if allowed to preach, they can birth souls
also into the Kingdom of God, especially enhanced by her
nurturing skills.

> The Rev. B. T. Roberts in his book *Or-*
> *daining Women* says, "Christ was the
> seed of the woman. Woman gave to
> the world man's Redeemer. If she
> was first in the fall, she was first in
> the restoration. Christ has redeemed
> us from the curse of the law, being a
> curse for us." (Galatians 3:13) [29]

We cannot, as women preachers, allow Satan to intimi-
date us. When I preach, I'm preaching as a door to life; a
door to physical life and a door to eternal life. A woman
preacher then is doubly equipped to help God accomplish
His eternal purpose. When women were denied the chance
to preach, many times she nurtured and raised her sons to
preach. She gave them support. She gave them love and
guidance. *Now it's time for her sons to love and support her.*

When our churches fight women who emerge in the pulpits, we are fighting our mothers, our sisters and our own daughters. That is a strategy of Satan.

🙞 *Women preachers are not the enemy of the church. They are on the Lord's side. The church has spent too much time fighting women preachers instead of Satan.*

The enmity of Satan can no longer be a stumbling block for us. We must continue to rise up like Deborah and be mothers in Israel. As a mother in Israel, she was a wife, a mother, a judge, a prophetess and general in the army.

I believe in these last days of God's outpouring of His Spirit, many Baraks will say to their Deborah's that they will not go to battle without them. I feel it is the timing of God to restore man and woman back to the divine order in the home and in the Kingdom of God. It is the hour for man and woman to come to faith, to stop living under fallen doctrine, and to start living according to divine order. [30]

As mighty women of God, God has also given unto us "...power to tread on serpents and scorpions, and over all the power of the enemy; and nothing shall injure you." (Luke 10:19)

Stumbling Block #5 - The "Isms"

There is neither Jew or Greek, there is neither slave nor

*free man, there is neither male or female, for you are all
one in Christ Jesus. Galatians 3:28*

We could write pages on sexism and racism in the
church today. It does exist. In 1847, Antoinette Brown became the first ordained woman minister in the United
States. It has been 148 years since her ordination and we are
still in America dealing with sexism and racism in every
sector of our nation. Dr. Warren H. Stewart, Sr., Pastor of the
First Institutional Baptist Church of Phoenix, Arizona,
preached my ordination service. The title of the message
was, "If She's Alright With God." His text was based on
Acts 2:17.

> He states: No, there were no women
> among the twelve that He called and
> named but nor were there any non-
> Jews, African-Americans, Hispanics,
> Asians, Europeans, Indians, Senior
> Citizens, or American Baptists! If
> we're really going to push the point,
> Jesus didn't call anyone by name but
> twelve Jewish males! And that would
> leave out a whole lot of us who call
> ourselves preachers! [31]

His message freed up a lot of men and women and
youth in the midst of that service. Regardless of the "isms"
that we allow to cause stumbling blocks, we must turn them
into stepping stones!

An excerpt from a poem entitled TWAS WOMAN says
it well.

Who hailed the first appearance of pride
And listened while the serpent lied,
Consent to be defiled? Twas woman!
Who by the temper first betrayed,
Infringed the laws that God had made,
And all the world in ruin laid? Twas Woman! Twas
Woman!
REPLY
Who failed to tell his new made bride
How Satan basely, foully lied
About their being deified? Twas Adam!
Who joined his wife in sinful pride
Although he knew the serpent lied
About their being deified? Twas Adam!
Who tried to charge upon his wife
The blame of his own sinful life
When God and man were set at strife? Old Adam!
Who ever since has laid the blame
Of his own follies, sin and shame
Upon his wife who bears his name? Old Adam!
Who nailed His Savior to a tree
And mocked His dying agony
Their Lord with thieves on either side, Not Woman!
Who when her plea could not avail,
Stood near the cross to weep and wail
While murderers drove the cruel nail? Twas Woman!
And when He bruised the serpent's head
And rose triumphant from the dead
What was the first word Jesus said, Twas Woman! [32]

Stumbling Block #6 - Lack of Female Role Models

For you have been called for this purpose, since Christ also suffered for you, leaving you an example for you to follow in His steps. 1 Peter 2:21

Many of my major role models have been great men preachers of the Gospel. I learned how to take what was imparted to me and then preach like the woman of God I was created to be!

Many women preachers express that having no female preachers to emulate has been a stumbling block for them. I can identify with them. But this can no longer be a stumbling block (excuse) for us. 1 Peter 2:21 makes it clear that Jesus is our example. He is our model.

❧ *Nothing is wasted. Everything and everyone that God brings into our lives is purposeful.*

The first women heralds did not have female role models. Miriam is the first recorded prophetess and Moses and Aaron had to be her role models. She was a leader to the women in worship and prophesying (Exodus 15:20-21). How did she survive? I believe when the Spirit of the Lord comes upon us, we minister according to His divine will and plan. We read in the Scriptures that Miriam was effective in her ministry and an example to other women. Though she made a mistake in her ministry by placing herself above Moses, she was still a mighty woman of God and a pacesetter. The Holy Spirit was her mentor and model.

Human role models are helpful, but have they flaws. Jesus has no flaws and should always be our prime example. I advocate female and male role models, for I am a product of both. Women preachers today should be flowing in more power, security and anointing than our foremothers that preached. We have experienced the Spirit poured out on us, enjoyed more education, and accumulated archives of women's testimonies to provide encouragement for us.

No longer will we allow lack of female role models to be a stumbling block. We will build on what we have. We will focus on Jesus our example, the author and finisher of our faith above all role models. We can use whatever our experience may be as a stepping stone by realizing we have access to the testimonies of women historically and presently. I was the first woman licensed to preach and ordained in a 102-year old Baptist church. I pray that I was an effective role model.

Stumbling Block #7 - Too Many Hats

Take heed to the ministry which thou has received in the Lord that thou fulfill it. Colossians 4:17

Wherefore, seeing we also are compassed about with so great a cloud of witnesses, let us lay aside every weight and the sin which doth so easily beset us, and let us run with patience the race that is set before us. Hebrews 12:1

A major stumbling block for women once they answer The Call is getting uncluttered in order to really do the work of the ministry. God had to deal with me for several years about getting myself "uncluttered" for Him. Women tend to have a multitude of responsibility with home and family life which is one full-time job, and then full-time employment outside the home. On top of all this she has the call of God on her life. The Holy Spirit reminds us to lay aside every weight, anything that would hold us back from giving God our all. And the Holy Spirit will convict us of sin in our lives that make our ministry ineffective.

I'll share a dream that the Lord used to teach me about "clutter." I saw myself in the church of my childhood. The church was packed with people. Someone came to me and said, "Jackie, you are going to have to minister right now." I was not prepared and was very concerned with what I should wear. I told them I'll be there in a minute. There I was in the back room, trying on different hats. I could not decide which hat to wear. In a few moments, the deacon came back and said, "You'll have to come now." I pulled off the hat that I had on because I could not decide which one to wear. Once I pulled the hat off, I walked out to the congregation and began to minister. God gave me the words to say. The words just flowed. Once I laid aside the "hats" of distraction, the things that drain us, the clutter, and the titles, I was freed to minister on the spot! I had this same dream for two years. Finally, after I had accepted my call to the ministry, I was able to interpret the meaning of this dream for my life.

God has called us to balance. Particularly for a woman in ministry, she must balance home, family, work, recreation, community and ministry. She is accountable to so many, yet God is calling her to Himself. I have found that God deals differently with me "a married woman" as a preacher, than He does with "a single" woman who is called to the ministry. God knows my limitations. He expects me to be true to my vow of marriage and family. So He arranges my preaching schedule, in light of my vows and responsibilities.

❧ *A single woman preacher will be more available many times to minister if she has no other family obligations (i.e., children). For the married woman preacher, God can use her and still be sensitive in honoring her marriage vow.*

I have experienced God for several months allowing me time to study and prepare and not sending me out to preach. I know He is respecting my family life and so when He sends me out to do a week revival or a ten-day trip to South America, it is not a hardship on my family.

❧ *The Holy Spirit is our managing agent. He will set our calendar and agenda if we allow Him. It's not how much you preach-but it's how well you obey.*

In summary, we can turn our stumbling blocks into stepping stones of victory by...

1. Not stumbling anymore over restricted interpretation of scripture. Study the Word for yourself, and seek revelation from the Holy Spirit.

2. Not being intimidated by rejection. Expect some rejection and learn how to overcome rejection through the blood of Jesus Christ. Allow yourself to be healed and then come back stronger than before.

3. Respecting tradition but not letting traditions that contradict and invalidate God's Word hinder us.

4. Putting on the whole armor of God as we battle with the devil knowing that "we are more than conquerors through Christ Jesus."

5. Setting an example for those bound in racism and sexism and any other "isms" that have caused us to stumble. Be an example in the Word, deed, in love and spirit of excellence.

6. Taking advantage of every opportunity to observe and be mentored by women in ministry since we are living in a time with a surge of women role models and team ministry models.

7. Uncluttering our lives and focusing on the priorities God has set for your life and ministry.

Chapter 2
Seven Assurances of God's Call

Without fail every callee wants to be sure, secure or absolutely certain that they have been called by God to preach. I believe there are at least seven basic and very important ways to test the waters. The order of these seven assurances may vary from person to person.

1. The inward witness of The Call (Exodus 3:11-12, Jeremiah 1:1-9)

There is really no way to prove one's call unless you have the inward assurance yourself. God does not give us a "Call Slip" or certificate of calling or put a seal upon our foreheads for others to see. The inward witness of the Holy Spirit is all that we have. Moses, Jeremiah and the Apostle Paul only had the assurance that "God was with them." Every preacher must have his or her own personal experience and commission from God. We can usually trace this experience back to an event. For Moses he could trace his experience back to the burning bush. For Jeremiah he could testify of an encounter he had with God had tender young age. The Apostle Paul can speak both of his conversion and call on the Damascus Road. When you have an inward witness it does not matter who believes you're called. What matters is that you are moving forward because you have had an unerasable experience with God and received your orders directly from Him and not a human being. Just as you were convinced of your conversion to Jesus Christ, your call to preach must also be a life changing experience. ?● *If you are not sure or convinced that you are called to preach, just wait. Before you step into the pulpit, you must have that assurance.*

In the words of an old Negro spiritual you must be able to say without a doubt, "I Know the Lord Don Laid His Hands on Me."

2.   Outward witness of The Call (Confirmation and Affirmation by Others) (2 Timothy 1:5-6)

This is an important aspect of assurance. What the outward witness does is agree with what God has already done. If God has called you to preach you will "reach" people through that gift. Again you must understand that just because one feels a call to ministry does not necessarily mean they are to preach. Your pastor, congregation, the larger church community, family and friends and even your enemies can be a confirming and affirming sign. They are the ones that give the outward witness to what God is doing. If God in fact has called you to preach, He will give you power and an anointing to "reach" people. Many callees can testify that before they even made a public announcement, the evidence was on their lives and other believers were already affirming them.

The Apostle Paul in 2 Timothy 1:5-6 affirms Timothy by telling him what he sees on his life and encouraging him in his young ministry. To affirm means to celebrate what God is doing in one's ministry. To confirm means to agree or say "AMEN."

> Sometimes people have been called and cannot get support and validation in their home church and find it necessary to go to another church, in some instances even another denomination. [33]

To affirm and confirm one's calling, others must be able to spiritually discern what God is doing. Churches, denominations and even relatives that have been blinded by traditions and sexism cannot provide a healthy support system for female callees.

In that case, the callee needs to determine if they can remain where they are. It may be necessary after much prayer and seeking the Lord to move to a church that can be a support system for your growth. This should never be done out of anger and rejection. More women callees than we care to count have fallen through the cracks and not gone forward because they were crushed by not receiving healthy spiritual support and necessary training and education. Let me say here that everyone's call journey map is different. Every callee does not go to seminary or Bible College. But every callee needs some form of continued training under a mentor or even a home correspondence course. Many pastors provide in-house training for their callees by offering courses in their own ministry schools. Whatever door God opens for your apprenticeship training and preparation for the ministry, callees must be expected to prepare themselves.

No other vocation, career, or job ac-
cepts people without some kind of
academic standard. Why should the
church sanction anyone not willing
to accept the rigors of preparation to
fulfill a calling that he or she claims
comes from God? [34]

There is a great need for pastoral care for women callees
in the Body of Christ. They have been discouraged and ne-
glected when it comes to affirmation and apprenticeship in
many churches and denominations.

My strong belief is that any callee, male or female, must
be given a clear "Journey Call Map" by their pastor, local
church and denomination. The diagram of my own journey
of The Call is to illustrate the general route that a callee
could take that desires to reach the fulfillment of their call.
From the time I was converted to Christ until I was ordained
was a thirty year process for me. Without the support systems and preparation systems in place, it is clear that the
place God has called you to will take much longer to reach.
In the chapters to come, we will discuss the roles of those
persons that can be support and part of the preparation God
uses to mold us.

3.   Divine witness of The Call (Exodus 2)

The life of Moses is a great study in the divine witness
that follows one's life. Moses had his sister Miriam and
brother Aaron nearby as he floated down the Nile River as
a baby in the basket. This narrative makes it clear that God

Callee Journey Chart

Conversion Experience

Divine "Call" Encounter (God & You)

You
(The Callee)

God
(The Caller)

Support System

| Family & Friends | Pastor | Your Church | Christian Community-At-Large | Midwives (Personal Mentors) |

Preparation System

Educational
Seminary, Bible College, Church Courses, Correspondence Courses, etc.

Experiential
Growth (Intern) Service

Ecclesiastical
License/Ordination Placement as Clergy

The Goal of the Journey

Fulfillment of Your Call

has "markers" or people stationed along our life's path to show His divine tapestry in our lives.

This may not be an easy method of assurance, but necessary and can be seen over a process of time. Anyone who has been called will be able to look back over his or her life and see a divine tapestry put together by God. I know that the "markers" God has placed along the way are divine clues to our calling.

Dr. W. K. Jackson, my childhood pastor, describes the divine clues of his sixty-five year ministry.

> "My sister and brothers who were younger than I would be my congregation. When Papa and the older members of the family would go to town, we would have church at home. I would preach the funeral for chickens, cats, dogs, and whatever. That developed the habit of preaching at the house when Papa was gone." [35]

For some of us "markers" represent people or places as clues to our calling. For others, markers may be those times we did "play preaching or practiced preaching as a child." My husband shared how he used to practice preach as a child to his siblings or he preached to his toy cars and pretended they were the choirs, ushers, pews and pulpit.

I must share here that as I look back over that thirty year journey of struggling and finally emerging, God placed many "markers" along the way. Most of the markers were women in ministry. For some reason I never noticed that I was drawn to them. I enjoyed being around them, following their ministries and befriending them. I had a sensitive place in my heart for how they were treated and even silently advocated for them. As I look back, I see that each of those women were placed in my life as part of a divine master plan. I can see how certain male pastors were also placed in my life as mentors and markers for what lay ahead. But most shockingly, some of my markers were "enemies." Yes, The Call will cause your enemies to be aggravated and rise up.

God even allows enemies to the calling to rise up and be evidence of The Call. Enemies are a definite divine witness to what God is doing because Satan recognizes the anointing and call before we do.

Markers are all around you. We just have to stop and look at the divine signpost that God has placed along the way.

4.   Prophetic witness of The Call (I Samuel 1:27-28)

The text in 1 Samuel 1:26-28 Hannah gives her son Samuel over to the Lord and speaks over him the following words:

For this boy I have prayed, and the Lord has given me my petition which I asked of Him. Verse 27

So I have also dedicated him to the Lord; as long as he lives he is dedicated to the Lord. And he worshipped the Lord there. Verse 28

Prophetic witness is a very special way to experience the assurance of your call to preach. Samuel knew from a young boy what had been spoken over his life. I always had a good feeling as a child to hear prophetic words spoken over me. My grandfather often spoke over me and I am sure he did not know I would someday become a preacher. He would say, "Snukkie," [my nickname], "you're special. God has something special for you to do."

I carried those simple words in my heart throughout my life. When things got tough, I could hear those words. That's why prophetic words given related to our ministry call is so important. It is in those tough times that we hear those words and can go on in the midst of great trials, disappointments, and testings.

What has been spoken to you? If you are called to preach the Gospel, God will arrange from time to time a prophetic witness to come forth to speak into your life.

☙ *Sometimes we are not ready for prophetic words. Be careful not to cast prophetic words down or take them lightly. Write them down and watch; for surely it will come to pass if it is of the Lord.*

I have talked to many women in ministry and they all can recall *prophetic words* that have been spoken in their lives. Some remember being told that as early as two years old they would preach.

My husband shared how at age sixteen it was prophesied he would preach. He could not figure out how the preacher knew what only Anthony knew. He remembered sharing with his mother (Mary Green) that God was calling him to the ministry. She then confirmed and affirmed him by sharing she knew he would preach when he was born.

She never told him but pondered it in her heart. When she was giving birth to him the Lord spoke to her and said He had placed an anointing on Anthony's life to preach. She watched for the fulfillment of The Call.

I believe that prophetic words come before we, many times, have the inward witness or confirmation of others. Then throughout our life, I believe those words are activated with obedience.

5. Endurance witness of The Call

And after you have suffered for a little while, the God of all grace, who called you to His eternal glory in Christ, will himself perfect, confirm, strengthen and establish you. 1 Peter 5:10

Being able to endure the many hardships that come with The Call is truly a sign that one has been called. What is bothering me most about "endurance witness" to The Call is the "quitting spirit" not only with callees but within the Body of Christ. We can't seem to endure any affliction, disappointment or discouragement. We quit as quick as we are called. I think this is a serious test of our calling. The Apostle Paul says that our trials, tribulations and challenges with the devil only come to perfect us, confirm us, strengthen and establish us.

Any woman callee who can endure the many persecutions and trials to fulfill her call to preach and still love God's people and flow in the anointing is evidence of The Call.

Let me say here for the sake of male callees, that I recognize that they too have struggles and hardships in ministry.

Though male callees do not receive persecutions for being a male, they do encounter obstacles that they too must overcome.

> A man in ministry needs a lot of encouragement. Someone needs to tell him what he's got to go through and how he ought to be schooled. But you know a lot of guys, especially if he's got a good voice, he thinks he's got it made. [36]

There is no shortcut to suffering. There are no exemptions for preachers or Christians for that matter. Persecution is an equal opportunity employer. God desires to develop character in us and a "finishing spirit".

Mike Murdock, in his wisdom tape series, *The Assignment*, gives a clear understanding of persecution being a clear indication of The Call.

> When you discover your assignment, you discover your enemies. Seasons of pain and woundedness will come with your assignment. Opposition to your assignment is the only sign you are making progress. [37]

We must expect to be tried in the fire as assurance that our "call" is pure and can stand the times of testing. No cross, no crown.

6. Fruitful witness of The Call

You did not choose Me, but I chose you, and appointed you, that you should go and bear fruit, and that your fruit

should remain, that whatever you ask of the Father in my
name, He may give to you. John 15:16

The Greek word for fruit in this text is *karpos* which met-
aphorically means works and deeds or the character manifested from one's life. But work is not enough to produce
fruit. That fruit must remain. To remain means that our
works stand, continue, abide or rather in the words of an
hymn "Let my works speak for me."

The Apostle Paul in I Corinthians 9:1-2 says:

Am I not free? Am I not an apostle? Have I not seen Jesus
our Lord? Are you not my work in the Lord? If to others
I am not an apostle, at least I am to you; for you are the
seal of my apostleship in the Lord.

An assurance of our "call" as we live out our ministry is
that our fruit remains. The Apostle Paul says that "the seal
of mine apostleship are ye in the Lord." *Transformed lives is*
evidence that the fruit of our ministry remains. Buildings we
build will not remain, but souls remain. We are called to
build the lives of people.

But more specifically, the fruits of the Spirit are evidence
that you are called.

But the fruit of the Spirit is love, joy, peace, patience,
kindness, goodness, faithfulness, gentleness, self control,
against such things there is no law. Galatians 5:22

This assurance of The Call cannot be taken lightly. Too
many callees feel they do not have to manifest these fruits in
their lives and ministry. Some callees remind me of the cartoon strip Peanuts. Snoopy's job in the cartoon required that
he work with people. The problem was that he like his job,

but hated people. Some callees go into ministry and forget that a true sign of Jesus having called them is being able to work with people and love them inspite of themselves.

A callee can be assured of their call by (1) the fruit/ works that emanates from their ministry. These works continue long after they are gone off the scene and bring glory to God and not themselves. (2) One major fruit of the Spirit that must be present is "self control". I am not saying a callee must be "perfect." I am saying they must be "striving" and "producing" good fruit. Their fruit will be evidence they are truly called. And lastly, (3) lives are being changed and transformed through your ministry.

7. Love witnesses of The Call

But now abide faith, hope, love, these three; but the greatest of these is love. 1 Corinthians 13:13

The Apostle Paul gives a lengthy dissertation in 1 Corinthians 12:31-13:1-13 on the "more excellent" way, the "best gift" which is love. Love is the final assurance of The Call. The preacher's ministry must flow out of the agape love, the pure love from above. Some might feel that I should have included "the anointing or power" as the seventh assurance. But we know that Satan can counterfeit and fool the very elect with his power. Power in ministry, signs and wonders do not provide the major assurance that your call is of God. The preacher must have the love of God. Out of the love of God flows everything that we need. The anointing, the power, the signs and wonders should flow out of the love of God. Where the love is lacking, The Call is superficial.

I have encountered preachers who "can't stand people." They forget that Christ died for people not positions. You cannot fool the saints of God for long. Pretty soon they will know by the "love" that radiates from your life whether you are authentic or counterfeit. *Without the love of God, you don't have a ministry.* In closing, all seven of the assurances can be tested against any Christian's calling to ministry.

Chapter 3
The Call and The Wilderness

> Upon my arrival in the wilderness, I
> met confusion, frustration, fear, sus-
> picion, loneliness, discouragement
> and anger. What was I doing here? [38]

For too long we have not understood that to "just an-swer" The Call to preach won't make us a preacher. I am learning that we grow in grace and therefore we grow in the revelation of our call. The Apostle Paul recognized this as he prayed in Ephesians 1:17-18

> *I pray that the God of our Lord Jesus Christ, the Father of*
> *Glory may give to you a spirit of wisdom and of revelation*
> *in the knowledge of Him. I pray that the eyes of your heart*
> *may be enlightened so that you may know the hope of His*
> *calling, what are the riches of the glory of His inheritance*
> *in the saints.*

Most professions have an apprentice period. I believe for the callee God has prepared The Wilderness for a train-ing ground.

The Wilderness is defined by *Webster's Dictionary* as an unsettled region. The Wilderness represents that unculti-vated area in our lives that need shaping. The Wilderness is the place we learn to settle all our doubts about our calling. The Wilderness included people, places, trials, tribulations and even victories. What I like about The Wilderness is that both male and female callees have to go through it. However, women callees encounter some extra obstacles just because of gender.

🍂 *I guarantee you that if any woman callee survives The Wilderness, she will come out smelling like a rose!*

The Wilderness phase is where most callees get frustrated and really need to pray Paul's prayer. Some give up, some drift for years, but hopefully most will come into the fullness of their ministry. Every callee at some time in his or her ministry must experience The Wilderness in order for God to develop them into His preacher. The late Dr. Sandy F. Ray describes The Wilderness as a jungle:

> You must not accept the wilderness as your permanent home. You must have a sustained discontent with the jungle. The jungle is the only route to the Promised Land. There is no alternative route. ...There will be fears and frustrations, handicaps and horrors, but God speaks loud and clear as we journey through the jungle. [39]

Why must every callee experience this wilderness period in their ministry?

🍂 *God settles us, cultivates us, and imparts to us in The Wilderness and finally launches us in The Call.*

Based on these four stages, one can discern where they

are in The Wilderness. They most likely are dealing with unsettled issues about The Call, or in need of training and
mentoring. Some are needing impartation of power and
stirring of gifts by the Holy Spirit by seasoned ministers to
"work the works" and be launched into the deep. For some
this "launching stage" could mean ordination, especially for
those seeking a pastoral or full time ministry.

🍃 *Male callees have less obstacles in the ministry and historically have gotten an "instant church visa" to preach.
But the Body of Christ at large is suffering now because
they accepted maleness as a shortcut for real preparation.*

I believe there has been an abuse of The Call by assum-
ing that one's gender and our cultural sanctions make one a
preacher. I believe in the last days we will see a purging in
the church and the "aint's" will no longer be able to stand in
God's pulpit. We all must be obedient and go through The
Wilderness God has prepared for us.

Many preachers are unprepared to carry the Gospel.
They have depended on charisma, a melodious voice, a
whoop and a holler, and even sex appeal. The tragedy is
that for many years some congregations would rather have
"an unprepared male minister than a prepared female minister." This is rapidly changing. Preparation and anointing
are becoming priorities.

🍃 *There is a wilderness for both male and female callees.
The bottom line is...no boot camp, no soldier, no wilderness,
no prepared preacher.*

Author Judith L. Weidman says:

> Women, perhaps because of biologi-

cal necessity have come to accept
pain more easily than men. Child-
birth teaches us that we must go with
the pain and not resist it. [40]

Women callees have to take in stride all The Wilderness
will teach her. Perhaps God has put in women what men
don't have, *a higher tolerance for pain.* Without this tolerance
for physical and emotional pain, women callees would not
have survived.

Bishop T. D. Jakes in his book, *Water
in the Wilderness,* sums it up well by
saying, "It is in the wilderness that
God weeds out the saints from the
aint's." [41]

This moves us to the text in Deuteronomy 8:2-3, in
which God tells Israel the purpose of The Wilderness. We
can glean some wilderness principles in this text.

❧ *The Call is only one wilderness experience. A minister
will experience other wildernesses throughout their ministry. For every wilderness there is a Jordan and a promise.*
Principle #1: The Wilderness will settle you:

*And you shall remember all the ways which the Lord your
God led you in the wilderness these forty years, that He
might humble you, testing you, to know what was in your
heart, whether you would keep His commandments or
not. Deuteronomy 8:2, 3*

We must settle "our call" with God. I first realized I was
in The Wilderness when I could not make up my mind to
answer my call. I had not said "Yes, Lord," nor had I told a

soul. I was still in denial. I was in The Wilderness. Then I attended a women's conference where Pastor Beverly "Bam" Crawford ministered. *It* was as though she was talking to me. Her message basically was to settle it. I was in The Wilderness. I had to decide to obey or disobey God's call.

I did share with Pastor "Bam" Crawford my dilemma. She recommended her tape series designed for women in ministry dealing with the fears. Those anointed tapes helped me to *settle it*! I thank God for Pastor "Bam"!

Abraham had to settle *it* before he could even leave for a place he knew not. Moses had to *settle it* before God sent him back to Egypt. Jeremiah had to *settle it* before God sent him as a prophet to the nations. Deborah had to *settle it* because all the previous judges were men and God needed her to arise and be a Mother in Israel! The Apostle Paul had to *settle it* and not try to rationalize why God chose him, a persecutor of the church. Young Timothy had to *settle it* and accept the fact that God could use him in his youth. Philip's four prophesying daughters had to *settle it* and not worry if people thought it was a "family affair." Priscilla had to *settle it* and accept that God would use her and her husband as a ministry team, something rare in those days.

I am sure I am talking to a woman right now in The Wilderness. You need to **settle it** so you can move through The Wilderness. Stop denying that you are called. **Settle it!** Stop being afraid. Stop being a coward, for this is not a ministry for cowards. **Settle it!** God's way is the best way. **Settle it!** Don't worry about what people think. **Settle it!** God will fix your husband. **Settle it!** God will prepare your church or move you. *Settle it!* God is Lord over traditions. *Settle it!* There is nothing too hard for God. *Settle it!* Stop making excuses. *Settle it!* Stop being disobedient. *Settle it!* Apologize for saying you would never preach. *Settle it now!*

The Wilderness was finally resolved for me on October 20, 1990. God had been wooing me up to this time and now I heard Him say: "You better get up! You are being outright disobedient!" I then went forward and stood with other ministers in the sanctuary. Although settled, there was more I had to untangle in The Wilderness. This was the first time I felt that God's tone of voice had changed with me. His voice had been a soft wooing, now it was strong and convicting.

Principle #2: The Wilderness will humble us. (Cultivate):

There is nothing like having to depend on God for everything to humble us. Israel had to depend on God for food, clothing, shelter, protection, water and even cloud by day and fire by night. The first thing we learn in The Wilderness is dependency on God.

❧ *When a woman hears The Call to preach the Gospel of Jesus Christ, she must hear it through the issues of culture, sexism, racism, family ties, motherhood, economic conditions, traditions of men, religious spirits and persecution even by other women. It's a wonder she hears The Call at all!*

The word humble in Deuteronomy 8:2-3 means *anah* (Hebrew), to submit self as well as "to answer." I experienced this humbling as a cultivation process. To cultivate something means to spend time developing a relationship or seeking intimacy; to take time to train and refine someone or something. In the wilderness of tradition and sexism, I had to learn to be content and proud of being a woman callee. In the midst of my marriage relationship with my husband, God allowed me to see that my husband and I were a preaching team from the foundations of the earth. The dilemma was that he was cultivated to preach due to traditions of our denomination and I was not cultivated nor conditioned for The Call. But we were both called.

In the midst of mothering my children, I realized I had been proclaiming the Gospel all along in my household but from a domestic pulpit. God was now grooming me and refining me to stand and preach from pulpits that had been stained with sexism and traditions of men. I needed to be in The Wilderness so God could prepare me for the persecutions that would come from denominational darts and persecution even by sisters in Christ.

What a miracle it is for a woman to answer in the midst of the many distractions we have listed. I believe that all those distractions thicken The Wilderness. She must learn how to obey God inspite of them. God lets Israel know that their forty years in The Wilderness was firstly to humble them. Forty years is a long time to be in a wilderness. Forty years is a long time to "be on your way" going anywhere. God forbid that it would take a callee forty years to humble themselves and submit to God's plan for their life. I spent twenty-two years in The Wilderness. From the time I received Christ at age nine, I remained in "limbo," unsettled, until about age thirty-five.

We know from Israel's history, that after forty years, a generation did die in The Wilderness and never inherited the Promise. There are many women whose ministries I say were aborted or they had miscarried along the way. There surely are enough complications and hardships that only women encounter.

Again, I quote Bishop T. D. Jakes' book, *Water In The Wilderness:*

> I want to warn you that you will have to go through The Wilderness to attain the will of God for your life. The Wilderness teaches us to stand; it teaches us to cast all our cares upon Him; to totally depend on Him for life support. [42]

My personal story in The Wilderness was experienced in a one hundred year old African-American Baptist Church. This was where God would prove me. My church had not even considered the idea of sanctioning a woman callee. Though they had received many women as guest speakers, they had not licensed or ordained women.

☙ *I can truly say that "tradition" can be a wilderness experience.*

When you find yourself in a wilderness of "tradition" you are walking on dangerous ground. It will take the Spirit of God to work in churches strongly ingrained with traditions. All God requires is that we stand, and the battle is the Lord's. I shall never forget after I had been licensed, standing at the Communion Table. I was aware that there were deacons who did not even want me to stand at the table. Some refused to take Communion. However, I was crying on the inside and saying, "Jesus died for me too, and because of His blood, I have a right to stand and serve." The moment was very difficult and I could have turned back. I was the only woman standing with the brethren. God was proving me and God was "keeping me."

Women experience all kinds of "trying traditions" in The Wilderness. Sexism can be a wilderness. God just wants to see if you are secure in being the woman He made you to be. Racism can be a wilderness. God just wants to see if you can stand under the pressure of prejudice and be affirmed in your rich heritage. Ignorance can be a wilderness. God wants to see if you can stand in their midst and "teach" the better way. I learned from traditions that you might be the only woman callee in your congregation, but if God can be for you, who can be against you? There were no women callees who voiced this call publicly before me in this church. But the Holy Spirit took me through that wilderness and taught me survival techniques. I learned to pray; I learned to love my enemies; I learned to stand alone but in Him, and I learned how unpopular this call could be. Yet, most of all, I learned that I was a "pioneer in this wilderness" and was paving the way for other women callees and my spiritual daughters.

Principle #3: The Wilderness will prove us. (Impartation):

The Wilderness teaches the callee that God is all he or she needs! Don't underestimate the power of wilderness living! God told Israel, "Now that it's settled that I have called you and you have come through a humbling process, I am going to prove you and make sure your agenda has become mine."

God imparts the proving of us at this stage. This impartation is the preparation we need. My impartation took several forms. Firstly, God sent spiritual midwives (other women preachers) into my life to nurture me. Secondly, God opened the doors for me to go to seminary and supernaturally paid my tuition. Thirdly, God also sent men of God into my life that opened their pulpits to me to preach and teach their congregations. Fourthly, I was mentored personally by the Holy Spirit, learning to discern Satan's tactics, developing a life of intercession, and experienced the awesome moves of the Holy Spirit's power!

Lastly and most importantly, I was filled with the Holy Spirit and my life has never been the same. The Holy Spirit must have time to impart His power to us to do effective ministry. We have many callees, male and female, who never received power to do effective ministry. In The Wilderness God desires to impart wisdom, gifts, and revelation knowledge so the callee can perform that which they are called to do. How does this impartation take place? The callee must spend intimate time with the Lord just as the disciples of the early church did.

What did God have in mind when He set out to "prove" Israel in The Wilderness? I believe He was seeing if He could trust Israel. I believe He wanted to see if Israel would obey His commandments. The foundation of any callee's ministry lies in the fact that they know how to "obey the

Lord."

❧ *God has never been concerned whether a callee is male or female. He is only concerned that the callee has learned to obey His voice and can be trusted with the impartation of the Holy Spirit's power.*

I finally understood "impartation" when I went to Argentina in November 1994. To impart means to "grant a share or pass on or transmit to another." There are some things we can only get from the Holy Spirit. Seminary training, books, conferences and all the degrees in the world cannot impart the anointing of the Holy boldness, or the wisdom that comes from the Holy Spirit Himself.

❧ *We must know Him intimately, depend upon Him entirely, and follow Him exclusively in order to minister effectively.*

In Argentina where pastors were imparting to us the Spirit of the Lord, I began to understand why we have so many "powerless churches" and timid ministers. No one imparted anything to them beyond human skills. Impartation comes to us in several ways for the work of the ministry. Jesus always called and equipped His disciples with the power to do the work. That's why He told them in Acts 1:8, "Don't go anywhere! Don't take any engagements! Don't preach any revivals until you get the power! The Holy Ghost will impart this power that you need!" We need to follow Jesus' example. Impartation came through the laying on of hands and prayer (Acts 13:3), the breathing upon someone (John 20:22), and especially by spending time alone in the presence of God (Exodus 3:4-10, Galatians 1:17-

24). Our churches lack the ministry of impartation. We must have Spirit-filled and Spirit-led pastors and leaders that have something to impart. Paul said:

> For I long to see you, that I may impart [Greek. metadidomi-give with a cheerful outflow] unto you some spiritual gift, to the end ye may be established." Romans 1:11

In order to be able to effectively implement our ministry, we must know what we are called specifically to do. Others should be able to clearly see the evidence and fruit of our call.

When God calls a preacher, he or she has a job description from the Holy Ghost. We have a general description for all who preach, but each of us has specified people and regions God will assign to us. We have a scope of ministry within the whole body. Traditionally, in African-American Baptist Churches, the female callee was assigned to Christian Education or was labeled an Evangelist. These two areas, whether she chose them or not, was her only entry to the pulpit. It is important for male or female callees to be able to fulfill ministry tasks designated by the pastor. Some of the tasks may not be in the center of their calling, but there must be an apprenticeship period and proving of one's ability to complete tasks assigned. One must sometimes do other tasks to determine and discover the center of their "anointing" in ministry. Truly, one's gift will make room for them. Serve as God opens the doors, but don't compromise what you know to be God's call on your life.

Principle #4: The Wilderness will launch you:

Some callees come out of The Wilderness too soon! You

can tell when a callee is out too soon for certain signs follow them. Signs follow the powerless just like there are signs that follow those that move in God's power!

Being launched means the callee is ready to go out on their own having completed the Call Journey Map for their own life.

Some signs indicating unreadiness for a callee to be launched

1. Callee is still unsettled about The Call.
2. Callee is immature and not ready to pay the price that comes with the territory of full time ministry. (i.e., opposition, meager financial, church conflict, woundedness and suffering for the sake of Christ)
3. Callee has very little good fruit that speaks on behalf of their life and ministry.
4. Callee is timid and foreign to the power and demonstration of the Holy Spirit.
5. Insecure and jealous of others.
6. Has not completed a time of preparation and apprenticeship.
7. In a hurry to be successful instead of just being faithful where God has planted them.

Kim Clement, a well-known prophet from South Africa, and one who has traveled throughout the world, teaches profoundly on the necessity of handling the Gospel.

What was from the beginning, what we have heard, what we have seen with our eyes, what we beheld and our hands handled, concerning the Word of Life. 1 John 1:1

There are three experiences you must

go through in order to bring or manifest the treasure that lives inside of
you, that dwells inside of you. The
first one we must experience is **hearing**, then **seeing** and **touching**. [43]

❧ *Before God launches you, you must be able to testify to
things you have heard, seen and touched for yourself.*

If one of these areas apply to you, you are not ready to
be launched "into the deep." You cannot take people in the
"deep" things of God if you are in the shallow. You've got
to let The Wilderness have its perfect work.

When God launches us, we can go into the deep. We can
say like the Apostle Paul:

*So as much as in me, I AM READY to preach the Gos-
pel...For I am not ashamed of the Gospel of Christ. Romans 1:15-16.*

❧ *The Wilderness will reveal what we are really made of.*

In The Wilderness, impartation of purpose, power, sub-
stance, vision, protection, direction, and deliverance come
forth. Acts 1:8 is a good example of the impartation that
Jesus had prepared for His disciples. He told them

*But ye shall receive power, after the Holy Ghost is come
upon you: and ye shall be my witnesses unto me both in
Jerusalem, and in all Judea, and in Samaria, and unto the
uttermost part of the earth.*

The upper room was part of that wilderness experience.
There they were, 120 of them waiting on the power. They
could not accept any engagements, they could not preach
any revivals or heal another sick person until they had been

endued with power. My strong belief is that so many callees are powerless because somebody (namely God's preachers) didn't wait in The Wilderness long enough to get the impartation of the Holy Ghost!

I would conclude that The Wilderness is not all bad! Yes, it can be painful, but as I studied the scriptures on The Wilderness, I began to rejoice! I began to understand that God needed to purge me in The Wilderness! I began to understand that you can't get the "wine until you crush the grapes." I began to understand that the reason I was in The Wilderness was to bring out the best that God had put in me.

There are some blessings in The Wilderness!

In The Wilderness of Beersheba, Hagar heard God's voice and saw a well of water.

In The Wilderness of Paran, Ishmael found a wife.

In The Wilderness of the Red Sea, Israel was led by God to a place of no return to Egypt.

In The Wilderness of Shur, Israel got water from a rock.

In The Wilderness of Sin, God rained down bread from heaven.

In The Wilderness of Sinai, Moses received the Ten Commandments.

In The Wilderness of Zin, the spies saw the Promised Land.

In The Wilderness of Judah, victory came to drive out the inhabitants.

In The Wilderness of Ziph, God hid David from Saul.

In The Wilderness of Man, David and His men hid from Saul.

In The Wilderness of Engedi, David spared Saul's life.
In The Wilderness of Tekoa, Jehosaphat called for the Praisers and won the battle.

How long then should the callee remain in The Wilderness? As long as it takes for God to prepare you. Stay until you to pass every divine test.

I say let The Wilderness have her perfect work. *Stay in The Wilderness until...* you have settled the fact that God has called you to preach His Gospel and minister to the people of God according to His divine purpose. Get your orders straight from God's mouth.

Stay in The Wilderness until... you know the Master's sweet voice and no other voice will you follow. Become so intimate with Him that your only desire is to obey His every beck and call. *Stay in The Wilderness until...* you are filled with Him. Let Him impart to you His precious Holy Spirit and allow you to experience the power of God in your own life. *Stay in The Wilderness until...* God releases you! Don't step out on your own until He has prepared a launching pad for you. Don't step out until He has paved the way for you. And thank God if you wait on the Lord, and don't rush out on your own, then you won't have to repeat that phase of The Wilderness!

Chapter 4
Male and Female:
Midwives to The Call

❧ *There is a need for pastoral care to women callees since many lack support, confirmation and direction from pastors and local congregations. There is a multitude of women callees in labor...just waiting to be delivered.*

Then the king of Egypt spoke to the Hebrew midwives, one of whom was named Shiphrah, and the other was named Puah; and he said, "When you are helping the Hebrew women to give birth and see them upon the birthstool, if it is a son, then you shall put him to death; but if it is a daughter, then she shall live." But the midwives feared God, and did not do as the king of Egypt commanded them, but let the boys live. Exodus 1:15-17

What in the world does a chapter on midwives have to do with women callees? It has everything to do with me being where I am in the ministry today. Midwives played a great part in my "support system" as I went through my "Call Journey".

❧ *I thank God for the spiritual midwives that whispered in my ear, "You can do it, push!"*

This is a short but powerful reference text to the duty and office of a midwife. In my research I found that the office of a midwife is relevant physically and spiritually. The midwives from the biblical times were understood to be ones that "whispered in the ear" in order to facilitate birth. The ministry of the "natural midwife" has almost been lost in our day and time. In the text we learn that the midwife's main duty was to "cut the umbilical cord and bring forth new life." The midwife was a "coach" to the woman in labor. As a coach she was one that trains, tutors, gives private instruction, prenatal and postnatal care. Giving birth was hard work. Though the Hebrew women delivered with little or no trouble at all, the Egyptian women needed more help. Still it was good to have a midwife on duty. We can glean several important spiritual benefits from Exodus 1:15-17 to help both men and women callees understand that God uses "spiritual midwives" today to help us interpret and sometimes implement our call.

Benefit #1 – Midwives preserved life and did not destroy life.

The King of Egypt had asked the midwives to do something contrary to their calling. He had asked them to kill the baby boys and save the baby girls. The midwives feared the Lord and instead obeyed the law of God. To preserve life is to protect life. I thank God for spiritual midwives that God sent into my life to preserve me. Midwives were there to impart wisdom to prevent miscarriages. Just when I needed someone, God's midwives (a seasoned woman and experienced woman of the Gospel or a seasoned man) would give me a word of encouragement. Just when I was about to give up, they whispered "fight on." Just when I thought I was the only one going through the fire, they shared their story with me. When Satan would have destroyed me, and aborted my ministry, the midwife wouldn't stand by and let it happen. Instead, they prayed me through and cut the umbilical cords of fear and discouragement.

Benefit #2 – Midwives prepare you for delivery.

Midwives spent time in prenatal care of the mother. This care was important for her body and built her confidence for labor. The midwife provided vital information necessary for a safe delivery. The midwife, unlike our modern day physicians, was called to provide crucial emotional support and spend ten to twelve hours with the mother in the labor room, rub their back and be with them as long as they needed. The midwife was anointed to minister emotionally and physically. She was a "troubleshooter" and knew where problems might surface. I shall never forget spiritual midwifes who sat up with me listening and weeping with me as my ministry was birthed.

Our pastors are significant as midwives. Without pastoral midwivery, our labor and delivery are very difficult.

> Without the pastor it is virtually impossible for the callee to negotiate the liminal state and move through the rites of passage. Although the community of faith helps to validate the callee, without a sponsor like the pastor the individual could be left in the

liminal state for a very long time. [44]

Benefit #3 – Midwives get you in a birthing position.

As the women sat upon the birthing stools in this text, the midwife was the first one to see the baby coming and determine what the baby would be. Labor is easier if you are in position. In the spiritual sense, many women have hard labors because they were not in the birthing position. To position yourself you must be in prayer, study of God's Word, fellowship with other women in ministry, under the covering of your leadership and listening to the Lord for your next step.

Benefit #4 – Midwives help you proceed with Caution!

In labor it is important to know when to push and when to "pant." Panting is labored breathing or marking time until you can push through. The midwife is there to instruct you how to proceed with caution. If a woman pushes too soon, there can be much discomfort and tearing that takes place in her physical body. There could be damage to other body functions. Our "call" should not destroy those around us. If we press our way or force our "call" on others, our ministries will be damaged before we start. In the spiritual birthing process of one's ministry, it is important to know when to push and when to proceed with caution. A woman must proceed with caution if the pastor and congregation are not ready to receive her ministry. She must proceed with caution when her own family members are rejecting her. Sometimes we have to "stop pushing" and allow the Holy Spirit to do some internal workings in the hearts and minds of those we are effecting. There was a time that I asked God to work in those around me to prepare them for what He was doing in my life. This could take months, but it is better to proceed with caution than to push "your way right on out of your church, marriage, or God's timing." God will open the way for us to "push" completely through.

Benefit #5 – Midwives help you push!

I shall never forget when I was in "natural labor" with my first child. There was a woman in the next room screaming. She kept hollering out, "I don't want to push, I don't want to push!" My husband looked at me and said "She's going to be here a long time." You have got to have someone to help you push your ministry through. A midwife serves this purpose. I have seen women in our women's conferences where the Spirit of the Lord would come upon them, and they (literally in the Spirit) would start having contractions in the Spirit, and travailing in the Spirit. We began to understand that in the Spirit, our ministries are birthed. The trials and tribulations get rough and we sometimes don't want to push. **But you must push! Keep on praising God! Push! Keep on praying! Push! Keep on seeking Him! Push! Keep on fasting! Push! Keep on trusting! Push! Push and push some more! Push!**

Benefit # 6 – Midwives help you perform!

This stage is what I call postnatal care. Once your ministry has been birthed, you need to be nursed along. In the natural, when you bring the baby home from the hospital, there are no instructions attached to the baby's toe. You have to care for each baby individually and use several methods of care. For the woman preacher, as a novice, you need continual instruction. *Just because you are called doesn't mean you know it all!* One must grow in the grace of that calling. Midwives can continue to instruct you, pray for you, advise you and correct you.

❧ *Sometimes even human midwives may fail us, but the Holy Spirit, a Holy Midwife, will never fail us.*

In our churches today, we still need midwives. Pastors are midwives. Sunday school teachers are mighty good midwives. I believe that the midwife concept (coaching) is what good parenting is all about. Every now and then we need to ask the question "Is there a midwife in the house?" I believe God desires that we reach our full potential. I believe that we need more midwives today that don't meddle, but minister! We need midwives that don't murmur but minister!

Over two thousand years ago, God sent His Son! I get happy when I think about how Jesus pushed us through the chains of sin, death, hell and the grave! For when we could not push our way through sin, when we could not get in a righteous position, when we could not perform based on the law, God sent Jesus to take our place on the labor table!

It was on Calvary that Jesus went into labor for you and me! It was on Calvary that Jesus pushed through and bore our sins! It was on Calvary that He suffered and travailed! It was on Calvary that He bled and died! It was early Sunday morning that Jesus cut the umbilical cord to sin, death, hell and the grave. He birthed my salvation!

But the story doesn't end there! Jesus promised that He would send the Holy Spirit! Hallelujah! The Holy Spirit is a

Holy midwife! He will preserve us! He will prepare us! He will position us! He will help us push through! He will help us perform that good work that was begun in us! The Holy Spirit is a **mighty good midwife**! For He will never leave us nor forsake us!

When everyone else fails us, the Holy Spirit will not fail! No matter what we go through, if we obey, the Holy Spirit will bring our ministries forth. If we obey, the Holy Spirit is always there to whisper in our ear, **"You can do it!"**

Chapter 5
Coupled in The Call

Two people are likely to have more
strengths than a lone pastor and thus
compensate for deficiencies. You
have respect for each other and for
what we each can and cannot do.
Variation in styles of preaching and
worship leadership are refreshing for
the congregation. [45]

We are seeing more and more *"in these last days"* a
move of God that is displaying "clergy couples" working
together in ministry. For many years, the wives of ministers
and pastors could not claim "partnership" with her husband in the ministry. Even if she felt a "calling", she was ac-
cused of "trying to take over" her husband's pulpit and run
the church.

❧ *In these last days, God is raising up pastors and their
wives as never before. Pastors and minister's wives should
not be denied the opportunity to minister because her husband is the pastor; but because there is evidence of a divine
call and the anointing to operate in that call. Clergy couples
are needed to help bring restoration to the Body of Christ*

and order to the families. It is a powerful ordained model!
I have chosen to address several issues that face ministers who serve in *"partnership callings"* with their spouses.

1. **What is a clergy couple?**

   Answer: A clergy couple can be defined several ways:
   a. Both husband and wife are licensed or ordained in full or part time ministry;
   b. Both husband and wife minister in the church while one is licensed or ordained and the other spouse is involved in lay ministry;
   c. One partner has acknowledged The Call and is working toward licensed or ordained ministry while the other spouse may or may not be supportive.

2. **What constitutes a healthy "team ministry?"**

   Answer: I believe a team ministry does not necessarily mean you are at the same church or doing the same thing. It means you are both called, both in agreement about what God has called each of you to do, both working together to help the other minister effectively. Though you may minister separately at times, you are still a team. As clergy you both respect your differences and similarities in ministry. This makes for a healthy team ministry. My husband and I have separate gifts and we have some overlapping gifts we share. We enjoy when we can team preach, direct plays together, minister to married couples and pray together. A healthy team ministry *respects* the *uniqueness* and *space* of each partner.

3. **How do I handle "my call" if I can't tell my spouse?**

Answer: It sounds like God needs to do some preparation of the heart in your spouse. God is sovereign and does everything decently and in order. He calls you knowing He has the power to deal with the other spouse. Look at the Virgin Mary and Joseph. God had to deal with Joseph separately. I recommend that you obey God, respect your spouse by praying for them and "stay" put until God releases you to minister. While you are "staying put" you are studying the Word, preparing yourself through school or seminars, fellowshipping with others in ministry and ministering as God opens the door. **God will reveal it to your spouse.**

4. **What if my husband does affirm me in my calling but because of my small children and other household duties, is hesitant to untie my apron strings? How do I assure him I can do this and balance my home?**

    Answer: Combining the careers of wifehood, motherhood and ministry is not easy. It should be undertaken by well prepared, courageous, and highly dedicated women. [46]

    Our husbands may have hesitancy not because they don't affirm us, but because they are our "protectors." They know that the calling will affect every aspect of our family life and marriage. To assure him, you need to be sensitive to his concerns for you and the family. Secondly, solicit his help and your family when needed. Make them part of the ministry and not an added burden. Share openly what is going on with the ministry and your needs. Thirdly, you must discern how involved you can become with ministry having small children. God knows what your responsibilities are and He will not sacrifice your young family for the ministry. Find the balance that works for you and be patience until you can be more released from home. It will require courage. prayer, and a "no turning back" attitude to fulfill you calling.

5. **Are clergy couples a new concept?**

   Answer: No, the concept is not new, but biblical. We see clergy couples in the Old Testament such as Isaiah and his wife who also was a Prophetess. **Again, rare but not a new concept.** We see Aquilla and Priscilla ministering as a team in the New Testament. I believe it is the ultimate plan of God to see husband and wives ministering together as a team.

6. **Where did the cliche come from that the church is the "second wife"? Is this biblical?**

   Answer: Nowhere in Scripture do we find basis for this statement. It is important to understand that the "family was created before the church." God never intended for our marriages or families to be sacrificed for the ministry. I believe this cliche has destroyed and deceived many clergy couples and congregations. Clergy couples must cleave to each other and live by biblical principles.

7. **Are there issues of attire that should be addressed for clergy couples?**

   Answer: Definitely there are issues of masculine and feminine differences we can address. I think that women ministers should be feminine, attractive and conservative (moderate) in dress, especially in the pulpit. I have found it helpful to wear a preaching robe because you don't want to be a distraction when preaching the Word. Different denominations may have dress codes but women are never to look like men. If you do not wear a robe, you must be sure no cleavage is showing, or your dress is not too short and exposes you in the pulpit. Many women cover their legs with lace handkerchiefs to not draw attention to their legs. The market for clergy attire offers much more variety to women in ministry. **I do look different from my husband!** I should look different! Each woman must decide what is comfortable for her. To keep from being offensive in your dress, seek the Holy Spirit for direction. Many times the Holy Spirit has given me direction on what to wear, especially to a church where I have never preached. He is always right! Men in ministry must also be aware of their dress. My husband mentored his young male preachers to always wear a dark or gray suit and white collar when going into a guest church to preach. Stay away from gigantic rings and excessive jewelry.

Also, clergy robes generally have bars on the sleeves representing academic achievement. Make sure the robe you wear is appropriate.

8. **Though we are a clergy couple, our roles are different in relation to family life. When we both have to minister, how does that balance out?**

   Answer: I realize I must plan more carefully and draw from the power of the Holy Spirit. I am expected to keep my marriage vows by meeting my spouses needs, the children's needs, and domestic responsibilities and still find time to prepare a sermon. There is no special clause for women preachers. Clergy couples can be partners by sharing responsibilities that would otherwise be traditional roles. Anthony and I work as a team. But I have to burn the midnight oil to give excellence to the preaching of the Gospel. The Lord gives me grace, favor and the anointing! There are no exceptions for women in ministry. God has equipped us and gifted us to do many things at once. Wisdom is the key.

I am reminded of a song that said "I can bring home the bacon, and never let him forget that he's a man!" I want to take that further and say, "In partnership ministry, we are both bringing home the bacon and can never let traditional roles and ministry interfere with the balance in the home."

9. **What are the spiritual warfare issues that clergy couples face?**

Answer: The most obvious enemy (Satan) will really pull out all the stops on the clergy couple family. We must understand that they are dually, doubly effecting the Gospel for the Kingdom of God. They are a prime target for Satan. But I am reminded from Isaiah 54:17, that "no weapon formed against us will prosper." That means that weapons will be formed, but if we live right and pray right, those weapons will not prosper. We must, as Ephesians 6:10-18, put on the whole armor of God to stand against the schemes of the devil!

The family that prays together, stays together. Family devotional time is not an option. It is a mandate for survival. A good book to read on battle strategies is *Battle for the Seed* by Dr. Patricia Morgan.

Another real issue here is the "destruction of our seed." I believe our children are especially marked for the work of God. Because of that family heritage, Satan really goes after the PKs (preacher's kids). We have found that suicide is one growing weapon Satan uses on PKs. He wants to wipe them out. He makes them feel inadequate, picked on and ostracized by the congregation and peers. We must watch and pray and discern signs of deception that try to overtake them.

10. **How should we expect our children to respond to "two preachers in the house?"**

    Answer: Children adjust and adapt to what we model for them. It is no different than that of two doctors, two police officers or two school teachers married to each other. They are both professionals and there are hazards and blessings to every profession. I remember when I was licensed to preach, my daughter said, "Oh no, two of them!" Well, what she was dealing with was the peculiarities, the schedule, the fishbowl lifestyle we already lived. I have tried to remain their mother and friend, and they know I have times of study, praise and meditation just like their father. Also, we have to be mindful that children have special needs and demands for our time. We must never let the ministry "rape" our children of the necessities financially, spiritually, physically, recreationally and academically. Two preachers in the same household have to work harder not to neglect one another or the children.

11. **What dynamics need to be addressed with the congregation when the pastor's wife acknowledges her calling and emerges to team ministry with her husband?**

Answer: It is important for congregations to understand the move and season of God. God is doing a new thing in the earth and part of that move to bring in the harvest is "team ministry." Congregations who are rigid to this change in their churches must be willing to flow with the change or risk having God move their Shepherd to a place where the team ministry can flow. I don't believe that there needs to be a fight over such an issue. The pastor's leadership ability should be trusted enough to move the church in whatever direction the Holy Spirit directs. The issues of tradition come into play here, but congregations must decide if they want traditions over the anointing of God on their churches.

In my experience with this same issue, I know that most pastor's wives are already doing the work of the ministry but without titles and recognition. Her emergence is inevitable where there is a genuine call. A time of corporate fasting and prayer is the best thing to do whenever God is birthing something new in our midst.

Chapter 6
Reconciliation for the Sake
of The Call

> It is not healthy for the body to have
> parts which despise the other parts
> no matter how unsightly. [47]

Thanks be to God that there are pastors and churches across this nation who have affirmed women callees for many years. This chapter, however, is not written to stir us to anger, but to bring us to a place of repentance or "sackcloth and ashes" for the sake of the Gospel of Jesus Christ.

Never in the history of our churches have so many women attended seminary and directly or indirectly articulated a call to ministry in our churches. Women especially bring a reinterpretation to this new movement in ministry. We are creating as we go along. The presence of women in ministry challenges us, challenges our congregations and our male colleagues to rethink ministry and the mission of the church.

Out of all the chapters in this book, the subject of reconciliation in God's pulpit brings up some deep, unresolved wounds. I can remember being a Women's Day speaker (at

the time I was still a secret agent) but I knew I was really going to preach and not just give a speech. Fannie E. Suddarth
describes the same experience as far back as the early 1900s
in this way:

> In due time the call to preach was
> whispered to my heart by the Holy
> Spirit, but I dared not call myself a
> minister. I gave numberless lectures
> and exhortations, but I shrank from
> calling them sermons until the sum-
> mer of 1903. [48]

The pulpit was full of men, no women. I sat in the rear
waiting to be introduced. It was apparent that women did
not grace the pulpit and I felt the pulpit was a *"hostile environment."* I was safer in the pews. Anyway, I did not know
where I was to speak from since no one invited me to the
pulpit. My eyes spotted a small podium on the floor and I
assumed that would be my place. I shall never forget feeling
such a division among the "proclaimers" of the Gospel and
what that image transferred to the congregation. I stood and
ministered the Word, but knew that the Holy Spirit was
grieved. "Reconciliation must come someday in God's pulpit" I thought to myself.

> Because of the vastness of the corrup-
> tion in our society, the Lord's work
> cannot be finished with just the male
> gender. [49]

Here I was in a church that was celebrating Women's
Day but not really. They had not come to the realization that

the work of the ministry needed both male and female gifts and calling.

I understand what it meant to be despised by male preachers. We could not even sit beside each other in the pulpit. I understand what it meant for our Lord to be despised and rejected of men. To despise someone is to look upon them as worthless, with disdain or scorn. There is a certain look that male preachers give when they disregard women ministers...a condescending look. Some will not even sit in the pulpit with them because it would be a sign of acceptance. Or if there are a group of male preachers in the pastor's study and you are the only female, there is a discomforting feeling and a hushness to their male jokes. It's the unspoken words, gestures and stares that let you know reconciliation has not come to the pulpit. This widespread feeling of rejection is felt by many women callees in the Body of Christ. I say it is time for reconciliation in God's pulpit.

Let's establish now that it is God's pulpit. The pulpit is symbolic of an elevated place from which to "tell the story." The pulpit is the place to declare the unsearchable riches of the Gospel.

&*& *God's pulpit must not be defiled or contaminated any longer by our social, sexual, ethnic, traditional or religious barriers.*

Galatians 3:28 is clear in declaring that "there is neither Jew or Greek, slave nor free, male nor female, for you are all one in Christ Jesus." Further, 2 Corinthians 5:17-19 makes it clear, "Therefore if any man is in Christ, he is a new creation; the old things past away, behold new things have come." All this is through Christ who gave us the ministry of reconciliation, that God was reconciling the world to himself in Christ not counting man's sins against them. To reconcile in the pulpit means to change from being foes to friends, from competitors to complimenters, from offenders to defenders of one another, from enviers to edifiers, from carnal to Christ-like.

❧ *In order for God's Word to have a dynamic effect, the world and the saints in the pews must see reconciliation in the pulpit.*

Reconciliation is not something you "read about." Reconciliation is something you live. Men and women clergy must make a statement in action by publicly and "on purpose" exhibiting opportunities to minister together. The Reverend Frank Green, my late father-in-law, made the following statement at my licensing service, "There's room enough in this wilderness for her voice to also cry out." What he was also saying was it's time to move over in God's pulpit and allow the women of God to proclaim "the message." Because of the limitations and extra pressure that women preachers come up against, we can understand Dr. Ella Mitchell's statement:

> We women are challenged to exceed the minimum and break down the walls of gender discrimination through excellence of preparation and practice in ministry. But by the grace of God, love and superior per-

formance may achieve our goal. [50]

Reconciliation in God's pulpit would mean that men and women callees would have the same standards and both must exceed the minimum and break down walls of gender discrimination. Both men and women callees must, through excellence, prepare and practice a balanced ministry. Both must minister in love and superior performance to achieve God's goal.

≈ Whatever spirit is ruling in the pulpit, that same spirit will also come upon the people. If there is a spirit of rejection regarding women in the pulpit, then resentment is contagious.

I expected women to be supportive and understand The Call. Many times they were just as harsh as men and even more vindictive. This is another area of reconciliation, jealousy of women preachers by women. The African-American male preacher represented everything to the African-American community. For the African-American woman, the African-American male preacher symbolized what was not symbolized to her or her children in the home. The church was one place she could go to see a African-American male in leadership and in the forefront. It is a strange irony. But the pulpit in the "African-American Church" is a sacred cow. You just don't see women in "that pulpit" and particularly the Baptist tradition. This "stronghold" must be broken. Any tradition that conflicts with the move of God's Spirit must be analyzed and removed if necessary. Also, there is a spirit of competition among women that seems to be on all levels in the church. The woman callee, however, becomes a prime target because she is more visible, and has an anointing on her life she did not choose but she must be allowed to flow in.

Pastor Vasthi McKenzie of the Payne AME of Baltimore, Maryland stated in the November 1991 issue of *Ebony* magazine that

> ...from the moment she stepped into the pulpit at Payne, she knew she was involved in something bigger than herself or, for that matter Payne Memorial. To me, she says, I was standing for all of my foremothers who were called to preach but never had a pulpit to preach in. [51]

🍃 *For women to persecute women preachers is to reject themselves.*

There is a unique strategy that the devil uses called "bashing." Preacher bashing can be defined as verbal rejection of one's calling to the ministry based on their worth or gender. There is no scripture given to encourage us to judge a person's worth. There are four forms of preacher bashing:

1. Rejection of the callee as a custodian of the community not recognizing their worth regardless of gender;

2. Rejection of women callees by men preachers based on a perception of their inherent lack of self worth;

3. Women bashing women callees strictly on gender and traditional biases;

4. Both men and women rejecting children/youth as callees based on age discrimination and assumption that

they don't know enough.

I say that "preacher bashing" must stop! We must lay down our fiery words and "evil eye" for one another and be reconciled in God's pulpit. God's pulpit must not be a battle of the sexes, but a proclamation point of God's winning battle over all evil! I say no more "preacher bashing!" We must reconcile for the sake of the Gospel for we crucify Christ afresh when we despise what God is doing in the other. Women callees must no longer "bash" men. Yes it happens. We are just as cruel in our words and in our actions. We must not allow anything or anyone to defile us. The devil has kept us divided too long. This strategy of the enemy must be uncovered.

⤞ *Satan trembles at the thought of "oneness" in God's pulpit. He knows we will be twice as strong.*

I believe there are six major reasons we must reconcile in God's pulpit:

Reason #1 – Not to reconcile in God's pulpit is sin.

We will receive the greater judgment. To reject one another based on human sexuality and to speak against God's anointed is a sin. Yes, God anoints women and men. Here I need to interject that there are whole denominations that teach against women preaching the Gospel. The Bible is clear that there are to be no schisms in the body. *I believe whole denominations must repent.* I believe that in the days to come you will see a crumbling of these unsound teachings.

⤞ *Where there are divisions in congregations and various denominations God will give them space to repent. Those churches and denominations that refuse to repent will come under God's judgement.*

For those who read this section and have problems with it, look around you and see what the Spirit is saying in the Body of Christ. Everywhere you look, God is placing His clergy couples and handmaidens in the pulpit. God is making a statement about the unity.

Reason #2 – We must reconcile because the harvest is ripe.

God revealed to me from Matthew 9:37-38 where we are to pray for God to send laborers into His harvest, for the harvest is ripe but the laborers are few. God is sending laborers, but they are women! Many of the laborers are women!

> Having both women and men share leadership provides an inclusive view of the nature of God. [52]

The Greek word for laborer is *ergates* which means a workman or field laborer. There were four types of laborers found in Scripture: firstly, the self-employed shepherd that supervised and worked over others; secondly, a laborer in crafts and trade; thirdly, one that worked just for wages and protection; and fourthly, the slave laborer or forced laborer. Which of these do you think Jesus needs to bring in the harvest? I would surmise it is laborer description number one, for they have the heart of a shepherd, totally committed and can have oversight of others. The last three types of servants are self-centered, working for the sake of money or forced labor.

ᶺ *As the Body of Christ ask God to send laborers into the vineyard. God is responding to our prayers yet we are re-*

jecting His answers. Why? Because those laborers are coming in the form of female callees.

We must reconcile in the pulpit because the harvest is ripe. It will take male and female, youth and child to preach the Gospel in the last days. Men, women, boys and girls are dying and going to hell while the church argues about who should preach the Gospel! Whom God calls to preach the Gospel is His business!

Reason #3 – We must reconcile for the Lord is returning soon! We don't have a lot of time!

There is an urgency to reach the unsaved in the nations of the world. Upon Jesus' return we must give account according to Romans 14:12. "So then each one of us shall give account of himself to God." People in leadership forget how the Gospel will cut both ways. We cannot reject one another and expect God not to judge us.

❧ *Judgment will begin in God's pulpit because more is required of the watchman.*

Reason #4 – We must reconcile or history will repeat itself.

Who's going to tell the pastors, congregations, and denominations that we cannot play "monopoly" in the pulpit?

As I studied the lives of women preachers since the early 1800s, almost 200 years have passed and "my story" of trials and tribulations sounds like my sisters of long ago. Satan has kept this war going too long. We have the power to change history and not to repeat it. This war has lasted too long in God's pulpit!

A decline in the pulpit is a sure sign
of social decay. And one of the iro-

> nies of the whole bit is this preacher
> and the politician become. The
> church's perennial task is to keep
> from becoming locked in the arms of
> principalities and powers. For when
> this occurs, the church is not free to
> preach the Gospel.[53]

Men and women clergy will have to reconcile to one another in order to write new pages of history. Susanna Wesley, the wife of John Wesley, mother of nine children even in the early 1900s, had a remarkably fruitful ministry yet her opponents were present. Amanda Smith, a southern born slave "was called of God from the washtub and ironing board" to the front of the Gospel ministry. With her simple Gospel message she held the people spellbound. Her ministry in America, Europe, Asia and Africa has been wonderfully owned of God.

We need a "fresh" revelation from God on how to function together in His pulpit and the Body of Christ.

What attitudes divide us?

1. Women see themselves not as partners but have believed teachings that men are superior and she is inferior.

2. Women tend to prefer traditional gender roles for themselves and their daughters. These gender roles are more the culture than the Scriptures.

3. Women resent "women preachers" for they feel they are tied to home while the women clergy live professional, glamorous lives.

4. Women are envious of other women having "power" over them.

5. Restricted interpretation and taking Scriptures out of context related to women have kept women in ministry oppressed and in bondage.

6. Male clergy feel threatened in their masculine roles because they do not see women as partners.

7. They (men) have been raised to be competitive but not with their wives and lovers. We must learn to compliment each other.

Reason #5 – We must reconcile because unity binds Satan!

❧ *Satan is terrified of men and women clergy coming together in unity! It will accelerate the work of the Gospel and Christ's return.*

The sooner we realize we are on the same team, we take ground from Satan. Together we stand strong, and divided we don't stand at all. I remember my husband preaching in a sermon:

> The church is the only entity that shoots their own wounded. [54]

In John 17, our Lord prays for the unity of the Body of Christ. I believe this unity should be manifested in the leadership of the Body of Christ.

Reason #6 – We must reconcile because reconciliation is our ministry!

❧ *God is going to begin to use some people we would least expect to proclaim His Word. Youth and children callees will become more and more visible. While we are fighting about what "sex" can preach, God will call and raise up children and youth.*

According to 2 Corinthians 5:18 we are told that Christ has given unto us this precious ministry of reconciliation. The cross of Calvary is about reconciliation. The songs we sing are about reconciliation. The sermons we preach are centered in reconciliation. The altar calls we give are for the sake of reconciliation. The buildings we build, and the crusades we lead, the television airtime we use are all because of the need for reconciliation to God and to each other. The gospel we preach is a gospel of reconciliation.

1. **RETHINK our position.**

    Search me 0 God and know my heart; try me and know my anxious thoughts; and see if there be any hurtful way in me, and lead me in the everlasting way. Psalms 139:23-24

    Create in me a clean heart, 0 God, and renew a steadfast spirit within me. Psalms 51:10

    We must ask the following questions:

    a. Why have we chosen to do things the way we do?

    b. Do our habits, behaviors and traditions bring glory to God?

    c. Is our way of doing things biblically sound?

    d. Do we now see our need to change?

2. **REPENT of our own sins.**

    If we confess our sins, He is faithful and righteous to forgive us our sins and to cleanse us from all unrighteousness. 1 John 1:9

    If My people who are called by My name humble themselves and pray, and seek my face and turn from their wicked ways, then I will hear from heaven, will forgive their sin, and will heal their land. 2 Chronicles 7:14

    Once we have rethought our position and recognize there is sin, we must be ready to repent.

    a. Repentance is a complete change of mind and heart.

    b. Repentance is to regret what you have done and the damages of your sin.

    c. Repentance is to make a 180 degree turn and begin doing what is right in the sight of the Lord.

    d. Repentance can be brought forth by praying and seeking the face of God.

    e. Repentance is changing our position regardless of how it makes us look in the eyes of others or what it will cost us.

3. **RETEACH that which has been mistaught or overlooked.**

That the God of our Lord Jesus Christ, the Father of glory, may give unto you a spirit of wisdom and revelation in the knowledge of Him. I pray that the eyes of your heart may be enlightened, so that you may know what is the hope of His calling, what are the riches of the glory of His inheritance in the saints. Ephesians 1:17-18

It is always difficult to unteach that which has been wrongly taught or misunderstood or simply overlooked.

a. Pastors, teachers and church leaders need to ask God for the ability to reteach where the people of God have had the Word mistaught, misunderstood or not taught at all.

b. It takes courage and skill to reteach what others have mismanaged. Ask God for the anointing when teaching on delicate issues requiring reconciliation.

c. Teach with the commitment to equip the Body of Christ with the whole counsel of God.

4. **RESIST opposition and Satanic powers.**

Therefore, take up the full armor of God, that you may be able to resist in the evil day, and having done everything, to stand firm. Ephesians 6:13

As reconcilers we must expect opposition and satanic powers to come against us.

a. Satan hates reconciliation in any form.

b. There will always be people in opposition to reconciliation, especially where the historical and traditional foundations are being changed.

c. As reconcilers, we must be bold in the Spirit and rebuke, correct and set in order that which will usher in reconciliation.

d. Prayer and praise are major pieces of armor that strengthen our resistance to opposing powers.

Though the pulpit has remained a sacred cow in many of our churches, Jesus never made it the focus of His ministry. He neither worshipped the pulpit and He surely didn't die for it! The most sacred thing to Christ was the soul of man! The pulpit was only the platform from which He expressed His love. The pulpit is an elevated position in which one stands to proclaim the Gospel. Wherever the Word of God is preached, it becomes a pulpit.

- Noah's pulpit became an ark that he built from scratch.
- Moses' pulpit became the edge of a cliff as he stood before the Red Sea.

- Deborah's pulpit was under a palm tree as she judged the people and prophesied God's Word.
- Esther's pulpit was in the king's palace and she proclaimed, "If I perish, let me perish..."
- King David's pulpit was from his throne.
- Daniel's pulpit was visited by him three times a day as he knelt down and opened his window to Jerusalem to pray.
- Shadrach, Meshach and Abednego's pulpit was in the fiery furnace.
- John the Baptist' pulpit was in The Wilderness along the highways and byways of life.
- Jesus our Lord's pulpit was in a synagogue, a boat, on the sea, or on the mount, and finally on an old rugged cross.
- The Apostle Paul's pulpit was in a jail cell, on Mars Hill and in front of magistrates and kings.

Wherever God calls you to open your mouth to proclaim the unsearchable riches of the Gospel, the ministry of reconciliation, that becomes your pulpit! I thank God I am free to preach on the street, or a stained glass sanctuary, on an airplane, a hospital ward, a high school campus, a mental hospital, or even around the kitchen table. *Wherever God commands me to proclaim the Gospel, that becomes my pulpit!*

Chapter 7
Ordination and The Call

&❧ *Ordination is the final step in the rites of passage. Ordination is the final rite of consecration to a ministerial office and bestowal of authority.*

Three years had past since I had been licensed to the preaching ministry. Things were going well and I felt my ministry was being received by my local church and the community at large. I was not thinking about ordination but was still healing from the fiery darts of being a licensed female callee. God however, had another agenda. I was headed for a season of final consecration and fulfillment of a ministerial office. My call journey needed further ecclesiastical sanction in order to fulfill the call that God had on my life.

What is the difference in being licensed or ordained? There are many callees male and female who accept their call journey but have no idea of the ecclesiastical sanctions that come with The Call. That is why the Journey Call Chart will be very important to callees. They can get a general idea of the long road ahead of them and can count the cost. Equally important for callees is to know what is expected of them as they prepare for their ministry.

To be licensed by your local church means that your pastor and church has recognized The Call on your life. Pastoral care for callees should provide a callee training period and at the end of that training, given an opportunity to preach before the congregation. After that a preaching license will be given. This license will permit the callee to exercise his or her preaching gift whenever the opportunity permits at the church or in the community at large. A callee must understand that the religious community at large or secular community may not necessarily recognize his/her preaching license. The license is an autonomous certificate recognized in his or her own church. It is not until a callee is ordained that the state, military, and the city recognize him or her as an official clergy. Many times proof of ordination will be required to work in prisons and hospitals, or work with the local police departments.

෧ *Licensing and ordination moves the callee to "clergy."*

Licensing carries some limitations. Because your local church licensed you does not mean that all the churches in the city recognize your license. It does not mean that other pastors will allow you to preach in their pulpits. Your pastor will usually refer you to other churches you fellowship with in order to give you exposure.

The custom of Baptist churches has been to fellowship together; also, to invite the ministers within their fellowships to each others pulpits. Pastors usually recommend their callees to other churches to preach. However, this may not apply to a female callee if certain churches do not have women in their pulpits. I learned very early that just because my local church allowed me to preach and respected me as a minister of the Gospel, that once I left that home turf, I had to walk softly and feel my way. When going to other churches, I waited to be invited to the pulpit. Otherwise, I sat with the congregation. This was not a cop out, it was wisdom.

❧ ***Just because you are called to preach, and licensed in your local church does not give you the right to demand other churches to do the same. You must respect other local pastors and churches even when they don't receive female callees. Don't take it personally; it's a work for the Holy Spirit.***

Being licensed by your local church is part of the ecclesiastical support system that is needed in our ministry. Depending on what area God is calling you to serve in, you may not need to be ordained. Ordained ministry is usually necessary when one is called to pastor a church, or be an assistant pastor, and their position requires them to perform marriages (in some states ordination is not required to perform marriages), administer the sacraments and baptisms. If a callee's field of ministry only required them to serve and preach without performing ordained duties, then a preaching license is all that is necessary. Denominations vary on the requirements for licensing and ordination. I am speaking only from a Baptist background and my experience. I know callees that for ten years remained licensed and then were called to pastor and received ordination. Still other callees remained licensed all their ministry life and served faithfully in their ministry area.

Again, it depends on "the need" for ordination. The act of ordination should not be taken lightly. When Jesus ordained His disciples, they had been with Him, He had trained them, He had observed now that they would need to be ordained because of the type of ministry they would have.

And He went to the mountain and summoned those whom He Himself wanted, and they came to Him. And He appointed twelve, that they might be with Him, and that He might send them out to preach, and to have authority to cast out the demons. Mark 3:13-15

This New Testament ordination service by our Lord makes it clear that ordination had a clear purpose and was accompanied by delegated authority from the Lord.

Ordination and The Call have presented special problems for women callees through the centuries. I shall not get into all the pros and cons of ordination ministry offices. (i.e. Pastors, Co-Pastors, Bishops, Priest, Chaplains).

It was my pastor, my husband, who asked me one day while we were cleaning up the church from some event, had I thought about ordination. I replied, "No, not really." He felt that it was time to pursue every ministerial capacity including sacraments, baptisms and weddings. I had many times carried on in his absence leading the services, preaching, weekday prayer services and teaching. He felt that the need would arise for me to exercise in those other capacities.

This began another tedious part of the call journey. When my ordination was brought before the church, it was not an issue of my ministry being made full proof of, but what does it mean for our church to ordain a female callee? Six months of debate, some petitions by those in leadership, many church business meetings, and a lot of self examination by parishioners. Now was a time for the church to search the Scriptures and their church constitution. Now was a time for them to call other pastors and get their opinions. Now was a time for us all to really seek the Lord!

I want to say here to female callees that many times God will use our calling to break down the middle walls. Sometimes I believe "we must stay put." We must go through the fire! I was not given a release to leave the church. I did not know what the outcome would be, but my struggle was more than personal. I found myself in the middle of a historical stronghold. God needs some of us female callees to "stand still" as He uses us to accomplish balance and reconciliation in the Body of Christ. If we all leave and run to churches that accept women callees, the rest of the Body of Christ will not grow. I can say now that I am glad that I "stayed put." I did have several support systems in place, especially my pastor.

🕊 *If God wants you to stay in a church that is resistant to female callees, He will provide a support system for you within and outside of the church.*

My choice was to pursue ordination through the American Baptist Churches of the Pacific Southwest and meet their standards for ordination. This meant that all my local church had to do was give me a letter of recommendation for ordination. I would then have to meet the ordination standards requirements of the American Baptist Churches.

Upon completing those requirements, a celebration service would be set and my church and the community at large could attend.

During this time of testing and growth, I found myself at another woman's conference. I needed to be spiritually fed and hear from the Lord especially on ordination. In a secret place in my heart, I cried out to God to bring things quickly to closure. I had no idea that He would speak so clearly on the issue at this conference.

All the women ministers were called to the front for prayer and a prophetic word was given to each of us. The minister that spoke to me knew nothing about my present struggle. Her name was Dr. Minnie Clairborne. She asked us all to tell where we ministered and what our ministry involved. When she got to me, she looked at me and said out of the clear blue, "You need to be ordained. The calling that God has on your life will require that you be ordained. Don't worry about it." At that moment she touched me and began to pray. All of a sudden I felt tremendous heat. My ears began to burn like they were on fire. I kept thinking, "Oh my God, don't they see my ears are red and burning." No one knew but me that at that moment the Spirit of the Lord had touched me in a very special way. It was that same fire that Jeremiah spoke about that was shut up in his bones. After that conference things just began to fall in place.

The church did vote to ordain women. The vote was by majority. This vote was about more than Jackie Green being ordained. This was an historical victory orchestrated by God himself. That night would go down in history. That night the door was opened for many female callees coming after me. Such a bitter and sweet experience. I'm glad God used me.

In the months to follow, I prepared for oral and written requirements for ordination. I went before a council of twelve ministers whom I had never seen. What an unforgettable experience. My pastor and the chairperson of our deacon board accompanied me. The oral examination was not long, but it was intense. I had passed the oral exam, the last phase, and was recommended for ordination.

A celebration worship service was set for October 9, 1994. I shall never forget that day. It reminded me of my wedding day; a day of making a vow to God that I would serve Him for the rest of my life. I would walk before Him and serve the people of God with my very life. Their worship service was truly a "rites of passage" experience.

Chapter 8
Pastoral Care and The Call
Pastor Anthony W. Green

In my twelve years as Senior Pastor of the Second Baptist Church of Redlands and husband to Jackie for nearly twenty-four years, I witnessed Christian men and women laboring together, as citizens of the kingdom of God. Gone were the barriers of gender differences when it came to the subject of prayer meeting, teacher's meeting, mission, choir or usher's ministry. Indeed, women were welcomed to serve on the deaconhood (assist with communion), serve as a church trustee, and be "chair" for the Church Expansion Building Committee. Moreover, the only time we had a major division was when a woman set her "eyes on the prize" by desiring the usage of a tool called the pulpit. The pulpit remained a "no no," in this one hundred year old African-American Church. Even if a woman had made full proof of her ministry and had excelled in preparation, the road to ministry was mired with in-bashings.

Different than many African-American Baptist brothers, I did not have an opposition to the woman in God's pulpit; I had an opposition to God's pulpit being in my wife. My opposition was not one of tradition nor cultural conditioning. It was the "dis-ease" of gender phobia. I equated my wife's call to the assumption that she would transform from the feminine to the masculine (as I had observed other female clergy exhibit). I was wrong. I was about to let a myth hinder my marriage and my ministry! She's all woman and she makes me feel all man!

That's why I'm indebted to Jackie for "telling it like it is", as she does at home, at worship and in service to her community. I can never pay for the silent tears brought on by traditional dogma, cultural bias or gender phobia. What I can do is support Jackie in her quest to bring down the walls of prejudice in the pulpit. Jackie has put the spotlight on the tremendous need for pastoral care of female callees. Female callees must no longer be invisible in our churches and denominations. We must recognize, affirm, train, and recommend them as they serve side by side in the Body of Christ. In joining her by writing this chapter ("What The Call Didn't Tell Ya"), our hope is this book will help both men and women callees, pastors and those in pews.

Some will surely raise the question "What should I do now (after I've acknowledge The Call on my life)?" In fact, many a callee may assume that things just happen naturally. I think some callees have waited on Elijah's ravens and brook for far too long. (1 Kings 17)

In this section, we want to leave a "memorandum" to callees coming into the ministry. In providing pastoral care to callees in our church, here are some practical "things to do" once you have acknowledged The Call.

1.   Be clear about your calling! When I was at Bishop Col-

lege, a student was sharing his calling to a fellow preacher. "I was in the cotton field. I was gazing at the clouds and that's when I heard God call me. God shaped one of the clouds to form the letter 'P'; and I knew He wanted me to preach. His friend responded, Are you sure the 'P' didn't stand for plow?"

Some people have entered the ministry because they couldn't make it in other professions. This is dangerous and is synonymous to being a hireling. Please take 1 Samuel 3 and the previous chapters of this book seriously.

2. Pray for direction as you submit your calling to a local church and pastor (see Acts 9:1-19–the Apostle Paul's conversion). Expect to go through a period of observation (accountability) and preparation (responsibility). Be willing to sacrifice time and pleasure so your training honors God (see Elisha and the School of the Prophets, 2 Kings 4:38). Dr. Gardner C. Taylor says it this way,

> …but if when you do well, and suffer for it, ye take it patiently, this is acceptable with God. Most of us discover that sermons are born of a mysterious romance between preparation and inspiration. The faithful preacher willing to pay the price in study and prayer and that meditation which is a sitting silent before God, will find rich reward for his (her) pulpit work. [55]

3.   Study and pray and read some more. (2 Timothy 2:15)

Satan loves preachers that are strangers to the Scriptures. Satan tries to hide God's Word because God's Word reveal God's will (Psalm 119:11,105). You'll need to have the Bible in one hand and a newspaper in the other; the newspaper will tell you "what's going on," and the Bible will help you discern an understanding of the times. Always have a pencil and pad handy. When the Holy Spirit speaks, jot it down and do not rely so much on memory. Read! Read! Read! Increase your vocabulary and resource library. Study sermons of other ministers; it is important for you to understand the different styles and forms of preaching. If you haven't already, establish a "quiet time" (daily devotion). All anointed preaching and any ministry we have, grows out of an active prayer life. Have a daily Bible reading plan and become involved in your local church's prayer ministry. Let your prayer life be your witness (Daniel 6). Daily journaling is another discipline that will help you in the early stages of your ministry and will become a life long discipline. Christian broadcasting (radio/TV) can also be helpful in building you up. (Avoid programs involving denominated, opinionated absolutes and social commentaries.) Also, the Bible on cassette (or CD) is a good tool for Scripture growth. One of my mentors wisely instructed me to begin collecting church worship bulletins and programs. This will aide you in understanding, comparing, and designing various forms of the worship experience. It also prepares you for being flexible in participating at different order of worships.

4. Begin to collect some basic tools for your personal library. (See 2 Timothy 4:13)

    – The Bible (have at least three different versions; King James KJV), Contemporary English Version (CEV), American Standard or New International Version (ASV or NIV) to name a few.

    – A handbook of the Bible

    – A Bible dictionary

    – A thesaurus

    – A standard dictionary

    – A complete Bible concordance

Borrowing from the words of Dr. H. Beecher Hicks in his summation of Paul's modern day response to the Romans, he admonished in his epilogue the following:

> Be cautious, my son [daughter]. Not all those with whom you come into contact are saints. Many will feign their saintliness. Likewise, all are not called to be apostles. Many will feign their apostolic calling. Let them hear the Word and, in faith, be doers of the Word. You are called to preach the Word. As I have written: how shall they hear without a preacher?
>
> To those who are called to be saints and to you whom they know as apostle words are worthy of the gospel we preach. Saint is not just a description of what you do; it is what you do

upon hearing and believing and accepting the love of Christ. That is
what makes us worthy of the name of
saints.

Be steadfast in your preaching to the
saints in Washington and everywhere, my son, because Rome is everywhere and Nero is everywhere
and Jesus is everywhere too.

Grace and peace of our Lord Jesus
Christ be with you always.

Your father and brother in the faith,
Paul [56]

Chapter 9
The Urgency of The Call

Hush, hush, somebody's calling my name
Hush, hush, somebody's calling my name
Hush, hush, somebody's calling my name
Oh my Lord, Oh my Lord, what shall I do?
(Arr. by J. B. Herbert, 1923)

In the words of this old Negro Spiritual, we can sense the urgency of God calling His people. At all cost, we must make sure we let nothing stand in the way of us hearing and responding to God's call on our lives.

❧ *Whatever God has called you to do, you only have a "season" to complete your assignment!*

Throughout the Bible we find that as The Call came to human vessels, it was never on their timetable. Whenever God calls us it is *kairos* time. The Greek word for time is *kairos* and it means seasonal, opportune time, unpredictable or out of the ordinary timing. *Chronos* however is routine or pattern we are used to following.

I believe God's call upon the callee's life is always a kairos time because of its urgency to impact future generations. Therefore, the call of God is never just about "us."

Every biblical model that I have studied that had God's

call on their lives, responded in their *kairos* time which ef-
fected generations to come.

Was there a sense of *kairos* time with Noah? Was there
an urgency? I would say yes. Noah must have said "Hush!
Somebody's calling my name! O my Lord, what shall I do?"

Noah built the ark because a pure generation needed to
be birthed. Abraham heard his name being called and went
to afar country. Why? Because God needed someone faithful to impart His promise to for the next generation. Moses
heard his name being called. Moses took off his shoes on
holy ground. God needed to prepare someone right then to
lead a generation out of bondage. Joshua ministered to
Moses and when Moses died, Joshua heard his name being
called. He had to continue leading the next generation of Israel to the promised land. Deborah heard her name being
called. Deborah rose up a mother in Israel for the sake of
that generation. David heard his name being called at a
young age. He had to slay a giant and preserve God's name
for the generations to come! Jeremiah heard his name being
called. Jeremiah prophesied and wept for the sake of a back-
slidden generation. Queen Esther heard her name being
called. She had to decide "If I perish, let me perish! but I
must save this generation of Jews!" I hear the Apostle Paul
saying "Hush, somebody's calling my name!" Paul didn't
even have a good name in Christendom, but he took the
message of Jesus Christ to the Gentiles, to kings and the
Jews for the salvation of the generations to come! There was
a sense of *kairos* about all this roll call of biblical models.

I hear Jesus saying as He hung on the cross, "Hush!

somebody's calling my name." Going to Calvary was a
kairos time! It was season for Jesus to go to Calvary. There
were many out-of-the-ordinary incidents and events. I hear
Jesus saying, "Jackie is calling my name! I know her generation has not been born yet, but I must answer my call to die
for the sins of the world!" Men and women callees must recognize the urgency of their call.

✍ *The implementation of our call will affect generations
long after we are gone.*

I hear the song writers Lowell Mason and Charles Wesley say:

> *A charge to keep I have*
> *A God to glorify*
> *Who gave His Son my soul to save*
> *And fit it for the sky.*
> *To serve this present age*
> *My calling to fulfil*
> *O may it all my powers engage*
> *To do my Master's will!*

The Call to preach the Gospel of Jesus Christ is an urgent
call. The call is not for cowards. No excuse will do. I see multitudes in the valley of decision. I call you out of that valley
of indecision. There is a valley that Joel speaks of in Joel 3:14.
Many are in the valley of decision in serving God.

> *Multitudes, multitudes in the valley of decision; for the
> day of the Lord is near in the valley of decision. Joel 3:14*

In the Book of Acts 3:1-8 we find what I call a job description or model for callees. If I were to title the message
it would be You Don't Have To Be A Wannabee.

And Peter, along with John, fixed his gaze upon him and said, "Look at us." Acts 3:4

As you press forward with urgency, remember:

A. People must be able to look on your life and see Jesus. (Acts 3:4)

We must get our lives in order. We must work on being a positive witness in our daily affairs and in our own community. People should be able to just look on our lives, be healed, delivered and set free. They should find hope looking on our lives.

And Peter fastening his eyes upon him with John, said, "Look on us."

B. We must meet the needs of people, not their expectations. (Acts 3:5)

"And he began to give them his attention, expecting to receive something from them."

Jesus gave the world what they needed, not what they expected. They expected Him to be born in the palace, but He came in a lowly manger. They expected Him to rule on earth but He died on Calvary! If He had met their expectations, we would be in hell today! He knew we needed a redeemer!

Thank God He met our need and not our expectations!

We must discern as preachers of the Gospel the needs of the people. They come to church expecting a big choir, whooping sermons, and a quick fix through dance or song. But we must meet their needs. They need truth, they need the whole counsel of God, laying on of hands and prayer, anointing their sick bodies, casting out demons or just holding them in our arms.

C. We must have something to give! (Acts 4:13)

...and they were marveling, and began to recognize them
as having been with Jesus.

If we want the power to minister like Jesus, it's not in the seminary or reading books...we must spend time in His presence! Jesus says to the callee, "You need to be with me! Spend time with me!" We must be willing to acquire the necessary training for that specific call.

In order to "work the works" of Jesus, we must have His power in our lives. The world is tired of the Church tabling the works, sitting on the works, passing the works to someone else! It's time we worked the works of Him that sent us!

That is the job description for callees! But what does that have to do with a being a wannabee! Well, I told the Lord, I didn't want to be a "wannabee preacher." I wanted to do what Jesus did and not wish for the old Bible days. He told me that I didn't have to be a wannabee! And I have been standing on Mark 16:17-18 since that day!

And these signs will accompany those who have believed;
they will cast out demons; they will speak with new
tongues; they shall pick up serpents, and if they drink any
deadly poison, it shall not hurt them; they shall lay hands
on the sick, and they shall recover.

Hush, hush, somebody's calling my name
Hush, hush, somebody's calling my name
Hush, hush, somebody's calling my name
Oh my Lord, Oh my Lord, I know now what to do!

Appendixes

Callee Study Guide
and
Ministry Self-Assessment

Study Guide
Four Ways to Use the Study Guide

Prayerfully...
This study guide has been prepared with both male and female callees in mind. Persons engaging in this study must enter it prayerfully, with an open mind, and seeking direction from the Lord.

Systematically...
The study guide should be used to enhance each chapter from the textbook. The questions have been developed to bring about deep personal reflection and small group discussions. All the questions require personal answers. In a small group, this kind of personal sharing brings deeper reflection.

Honestly...
When She Hears The Call textbook and study guide are tools the Holy Spirit will use to help callees address where they are honestly in ministry. It is important to use the study guide honestly, especially with the self assessment.

Expectantly...
Lastly, the study guide can be a way to bring reconciliation in God's pulpit. The study guide is designed to help both men and

women callee's identify, interpret and implement their call. The questions cause dialogue among male and female callees to help facilitate reconciliation. The guide will also help pastors and congregations rethink and move toward reconciliation.

Introduction
Understanding The Call

(Read 1 Samuel 3)

1. *In* your own words, in context of the Scripture in 1 Samuel 3, "The Call" can be defined as:

2. Briefly describe your conversion experience (date, time, place). This is when one's journey with Christ begins. Conversion is the "activation" and "unfolding" of one's call.

3. Sometimes we do not hear clearly God's voice and Call on our lives. Describe the "hearing aids" that helped you discern God's voice.

4. At what age, or time in your life did you first "sense" God calling you to preach?

5. At what point did you feel "compelled" to preach the Gospel and "couldn't help it?"

6. With whom did you first acknowledge The Call upon your life? How did you make a public acknowledgment? What were some issues that you wrestled with in sharing it with others?

7. As a woman entering ministry, list three major hindrances to accepting The Call of God in your life.

8. List three hindrances that male preachers might face as they accept The Call of God on their lives.

9. Why is it so important to be able to identify The Call of God on your life?

10. Discuss ways you would suggest that pastors and churches assist male and female callees.

More Reflections

🍃 *Spend some time thanking God that He called you. Read Psalm 139, Romans 1:15-16 and Jeremiah 1:4-10.*

🍃 *Make a commitment to journal regularly as you watch God unfold your ministry. Log people, places, times/events, dreams/prophecies, and special events that point to God's divine plan for you.*

Chapter 1
Stumbling Blocks of The Call

1. What can pastors and local churches do to correct years of teaching in error regarding women in ministry?

2. What has been your interpretation of 1 Timothy 2:11-12? How will you pass on this scripture to future generations of our sons and daughters?

3. In what ways can we bring healing to women in ministry who have experienced rejection from the Body of Christ?

4. What kinds of traditions have affected The Call in your life? How do we overcome traditions that deny that the power of God is working in the lives of women callees (family traditions, church traditions, cultural traditions, denominational traditions etc.)?

5. How would you define a "religious spirit?" Does this spirit hinder what God wants to do in your ministry? Give an example of how Jesus dealt with the Pharisees in His time. Reflect or discuss Matthew 15:1-8.

6. How is the female callee doubly equipped to minister life? Why has the "serpent", the devil, spent centuries trying to discredit the woman as life giver and minister of the Gospel? (Genesis 3:15)

7. Nothing is wasted in our lives. Every experience can be used by God to bring about His purpose. Share some of the fragments or broken pieces in your life that have been "brick builders" for your ministry. (Romans 8:26-31)

8. It is important to get "uncluttered" in order to fulfill The Call. List some of the "hats" you may be wearing that are cluttering the way for your ministry.

9. What are the (1) advantages, (2) limitations, (3) precautions of being a single male/female callee?

10. What are the (1) advantages, (2) limitations, (3) precautions of being a married male/female callee?

11. List names of male and female role models that have impacted your ministry development. (Close or at a distance.)

More Reflections

❧ *Spend time in prayer thanking God that stumbling blocks are becoming stepping stones in your life. (1 Timothy 4:12-16)*

Chapter 2
Seven Assurances of The Call

1. As a callee, certain assurances of your call are important.
    Respond honestly to the list below. Check off what as-
    surances you have.

    a. The Inward Witness of The Call

    _____ Yes   _____ No   _____ Somewhat

    b. The Outward Witness of The Call

    _____ Yes   _____ No   _____ Somewhat

    c. Divine Witness of The Call

    _____ Yes   _____ No   _____ Somewhat

    d. Prophetic Witness of The Call

    _____ Yes   _____ No   _____ Somewhat

    e. Endurance Witness of The Call

    _____ Yes   _____ No   _____ Somewhat

    f. Fruitful Witness of The Call

    _____ Yes   _____ No   _____ Somewhat

    g. Love Witness of The Call

    _____ Yes   _____ No   _____ Somewhat

2. Discuss why it is important for a callee to "wait" if they are not sure they are called to preach.

3. What are reasons that female callees have problems getting validation from their pastors, churches or denominations?

4. What are reasons that male callees have problems getting validation from their pastors, churches or denominations?

5. If you were to draw your Journey Call Chart, what would it look like?

6. What enemies have you had to deal with since identifying The Call of God in your life?

7. Share any prophetic words that have been spoken over your life that confirm The Call in your life.

8. What kind of fruit is presently evident in your life that confirms The Call on your life?

❧ *Keep a spiritual journal of the assurances that begin to surface. Be watchful and alert as God speaks to you. (Colossians 4:17)*

Chapter 3
The Call and The Wilderness

(Read Deuteronomy 8:2,3)

1. Define wilderness in your own words.

2. Share one experience that could definitely be called a "wilderness" time for you. Categorize it as a settling time, cultivating time, impartation time, or launching time.

3. List some shortcuts that callees try to take instead of going through The Wilderness. Jeremiah 1:5-6, Jonah 1:3)

4. Share at least three things that God desires to teach us in The Wilderness. (Deuteronomy. 8:2,3)

5. The Wilderness is an "equal opportunity employer for both men and women callees." Discuss this statement in light of gender roles and ministry expectations.

More Reflections

❧ *Pray about the areas in your ministry that for you are not effective. Thank God that He will "perfect those things that concern you." Read Psalms 138:8.*

❧ *If you are yet in The Wilderness, give God praise that He is only proving you, testing you and humbling you. Find a prayer partner to help pray with you as you go through The Wilderness.*

Chapter 4
Male and Female:
Midwives to The Call

(Read Exodus 1:15-17)

1. Define the ministry of the midwife.

2. List persons who have been midwives in birthing your ministry.

3. How should a pastor perform as a "midwife" for a callee?

4. Describe the labor and delivery of your ministry.(Some women or men have hard or easy labor and delivery.)

5. How does our relationship with our pastor, local church or denomination affect our labor and delivery? Explain why it is important to have their support.

6. Share the kinds of "spiritual prenatal care" we need to get into the birthing position.

7. Are you being a midwife to someone at this time? If so, share some of your techniques.

8. If a callee is not getting the support system they need, what kinds of things can they do to get help?

More Reflections

❧ *If it hadn't been for spiritual midwives, where would we be? Read Psalm 124. If it hadn't been for the Holy Spirit where would we be? Give thanks for the work of the Holy Spirit as a Holy Midwife.*

❧ *Reflect on the times that you didn't think you would make it through. Share the Scriptures that became life and "rhema" to you during those difficult times.*

Chapter 5
Coupled in The Call

1. Define healthy "team ministry" in your own words.

2. Write down the names of three clergy couples that have been models in your life. How do they compliment each other and how do they bless the Body of Christ?

3. What are some of the hindrances or myths that local churches may have regarding husband and wife teams? Regarding pastor and co-pastor?

4. How has the congregation being termed as the "Second Wife" hindered clergy marriages? How can congregations and clergy help to correct this? (Genesis 2:24, Matthew 19:5-6, Ephesians 5:25)

5. List the strengths that clergy couples bring to the Body of Christ.

6. How does a woman preacher handle jealousy from her spouse (i.e. if it seems she preaches more, travels more etc.)?

7. Read Judges 4-5. This is an unusual case where a clergy couple functions in the Old Testament. Deborah was in the ruling position, but her husband Lapidoth was supportive. Discuss the dynamics of this clergy couple in biblical times. What lessons do we learn from Deborah, a wife, a judge, a prophetess, a singer, a mother in Israel?

8. What kind of pressures and special needs do PKs (preacher's kids) have that other children do not have in the congregation? When both parents are preachers?

9. What special precautions should clergy couples be aware of in rearing their children? Make up three commandments you would list as important for clergy couples.

More Reflections

❧ *Be thankful that God is using couples to accomplish His purpose. If you are a clergy couple or know such couples, take time to regularly pray for them. Satan has targeted them especially because they are dually effective for the Kingdom of God.*

Chapter 6
Reconciliation for
The Sake of The Call

1. Define the ministry of reconciliation in your own words.

2. Why is it important now (in the last days) for reconciliation to take place in God's pulpit?

3. What kind of things have defiled/contaminated the pulpit of God? What can we do to bring about cleansing? (2 Chronicles 7:14-15, Psalms 51:6-17)

4. Share how "what goes on in the pulpit" has power over the people in the pews. (Give examples.)

5. Discuss what it means for "women to persecute women callees, because in essence she is persecuting herself?"

6. Discuss ways that we can eliminate "preacher bashing" among men and women clergy. What is the root of all "bashing?" (James 4:1, 7-12)

7. How can we help whole denominations and congregations who are "anti-women" callees bring about reconciliation in God's pulpit? (Isaiah 58:6-8, John 17:20-23)

8. What can we do to bridge this "gap of contention" be-
    tween male and female preachers for future genera-
    tions? What attitudes and truth do we want to pass on
    to our sons and daughters? (Galatians 3:28-29, Acts 2:17-
    18)

9. List the reasons you feel the Body of Christ must recon-
    cile in the pulpit.

More Reflections

❧ *Take time to fast and pray regarding repentance and reconciliation in God's pulpit. Ask God to show you what you
can do to make a difference.*

❧ *Pray now for future generations that must carry the Gospel. Pray they don't stumble like past generations and that
the bitter roots of rejection and schism will be overcome in
the pulpit.*

❧ *Regularly take spiritual authority over evil forces that
seek to bring division in the body.*

❧ *Make a prayer list of persons, churches and denominations that need special prayer in the area of reconciliation
in the pulpit for the sake of the upbuilding of God's kingdom.*

Chapter 7
Ordination and The Call

1. Discuss the steps necessary for a callee to be licensed and ordained in you denomination or church.

    a. To be licensed a callee must

    b. To be ordained a callee must

3. What issues do denominations and churches wrestle with when it come to ordination of women?

4. What issues do denominations and congregations wrestle with when women are ordained and purse the pastorate?

5. Create and write out your own licensing service and an ordination service. Discuss distinct differences and similarities in the service.

More Reflections

❧ *Read Luke 6:12-16, Matthew 10:1-8 and reflect on the ordination service of the twelve apostles. How can this be a model for ministry for us today in ordained ministry?*

Chapter 8
Pastoral Care and The Call

1. What fears do men have about women callees in general?

2. In what ways do male pastors and male preachers struggle when their wives emerge to the pulpit?

3. Discuss the issues that rock tradition when the term co-pastor is mentioned.

4. Why have women callees felt they had to become masculine to be accepted by the Body of Christ? (Masculine
   in preaching style or even dress and how they relate to
   the congregation)

5. What kinds of fears do denominations wrestle with who
   have held strong views against female callees emerging?

6. Share ways that pastoral care can be more effective for
   women callees.

7. Have female preachers been role models for men? For
   you?

More Reflections...

ॐ *Spend time praying for women callees that have been wounded.*

ॐ *Spend time praying for a spirit of reconciliation in God's pulpit and through the Body of Christ.*

Chapter 9
The Urgency of The Call

1. You only have a season to complete your assignment.
    What is your assignment? Are you about the Father's
    business? (Luke 2:49, Colossians 4:17)

2. How does your ministry affect future generations? God
    is a God of generational thinking. What inheritance are
    you leaving behind?

3. What excuses have you made about your assignment
    (ministry) being incomplete? List those excuses. Re-
    member The Call is an urgent call. No excuses will do!
    (Joel 3:14)

4. What has the Holy Spirit imparted to you already to make you more effectual in your ministry? What do you need imparted by the Holy Spirit that you are lacking?

5. Define your scope of ministry. See the Apostle Paul's description of his scope of ministry in Acts 9:15-16.

6. Explain "You cannot impart to others what you don't have yourself."

7. Make a to do list of things you need to begin doing in order to move toward The Call.

8. The Call is an urgent call. One day we must give an account. List some of the burdens in your ministry that you know God has assigned to you to complete.

More Reflections...

ॐ *Share with someone or your group the urgency you feel about The Call.*

ॐ *Confess the sin of procrastination and disobedience.*

Ministry Self Assessment

Date _____ Name _____

Directions: Enlarge and make copies of this form and do an annual assessment of your ministry progress. This form can be used for clergy and lay persons seeking to assess their ministry strengths and weaknesses. This form can also be used in the pastoral care of callees assessing where they are in their callee journey.

Personal Journal

1. My Ministry Statement (Purpose).

(Statement should not exceed 3 to 4 lines and you should have a scripture foundation for your ministry calling.)

_____

_____

_____

_____

_____

2. My spiritual gifts and talents (List those gifts and natural talents you have).

_____

_____

_____

_____

_____

_____

_____

3. I am doing the following tasks which support my ministry statement. (Example: teaching four Bible studies per week.)

_____

_____

_____

_____

_____

_____

4. I have identified my ministry in the five fold ministries
    or other areas: (Ephesians 4:11-12 and 1 Corinthians
    12:28) (Check areas).

Apostle   _____   Miracles   _____

Prophet   _____   Gifts of Healing   _____

Teacher   _____   Helps   _____

Evangelist   _____   Governments   _____

Pastor   _____   Diversities of Tongues   _____

Other   _____

Challenges

5. I feel that God is stretching me, enlarging and sharpen-
    ing my skills in the following ways. (Luke 12:48)

_____

_____

_____

_____

_____

_____

_____

_____

6. My Daily Spiritual Diet.

(Check those that apply daily or regularly.)

Quiet time	___	Praise/Worship	___	Fasting	___
Prayer Life	___	Fellowship	___	Retreats	___
Bible reading	___	Witnessing	___	Revivals	___
Bible study	___	Journaling	___	Other	___

7. Educational Growth.

We never stop learning. What are you doing to equip yourself through college, seminary, seminars, home study courses, retreats, travel etc.?

_____

_____

_____

_____

8. Tools For Ministry.

Are you developing your personal library of ministry books, tapes, etc.? List or note what you have added this year.

_____

_____

_____

_____

9. Ministry Mentors.

List names of those who are personally mentoring you in the ministry.

_____

_____

_____

10. Record Of Dreams, Visions, Prophecies.

Share any dreams, visions, or prophecies that have made a significant impact on your life this year. These should be recorded in your journal.

1. _____

2. _____

3. _____

4. _____

11. For callees, list what you are presently doing toward completing requirements to be licensed or ordained or any other type of certification for ministry.

_____

_____

_____

12. List names of personal prayer partners you have and persons you are accountable to for spiritual decisions and actions you make.

_____

_____

_____

_____

13. List areas of Spiritual Battle and strongholds in your life.

1. _____

2. _____

3. _____

4. _____

5. _____

6. _____

7. _____

14. List Personal Prayer Needs.

_____

_____

_____

Suggested Reading List

Bristow, John, *What Paul Really Said About Women*, Harper-Collins Publishers, New York, New York, 1991

Buckingham, Jamie, *Daughter of Destiny, Kathryn Kuhlman... Her Story*, Gwent, UK: Valley Books, 1976.

Claiborne, Minnie, *Women In Ministry-How To Be A Winner*, Shippenburg, Pennsylvania: Companion Press, 1983.

Cook, Suzan D. Johnson, *Sister To Sister Devotions For And From African American Women*, Valley Forge, Pennsylvania: Judson Press, 1995.

Demarest, Victoria Booth, *Sex And Spirit: God, Woman & Ministry*, Florida: Valknrie Press, 1977.

Edwards, Jefferson, *The Call Of God*, Bakersfield: CA Pneuma Life Publishing, 1993.

Van Der Geest, Hans, *Presence In The Pulpit*, Atlanta: John Knox Press, 1978.

Hicks, H. Beecher, *Images Of The Black Preacher*, Valley Forge, Pennsylvania: Judson Press, 1977.

Hunter, Fannie McDowell, *Women Preachers*, Kentucky: Berachah Printing, 1905.

Jackson, W.K , *I Let The Lord Do It*, Oklahoma City, Oklahoma: Campbell Road Press, 1994.

Jones, William Augustus, *Responsible Preaching*, Morriston, New Jersey: Aaron Press, 1989.

King, D.E., *Preaching To Preachers*, Warminister, Pennsylvania: Neibauer Press, 1984.

Massey, James Earl, *The Responsible Pulpit*, Anderson, Indiana: Warner Press, 1974.

McKenzie, Vashti M., *Not Without A Struggle: Leadership Development for African-American Women in Ministry*, United Church Press, Cleveland, Ohio, 1996

McPherson, Aimee Semple, *The Story Of My Lift*, Waco, Texas: Word Books, 1973.

Mitchell, ED., Ella Pearson, *Those Preaching Women, Volume I*, Valley Forge, Pennsylvania: Judson Press, 1985.

_____, *Those Preaching Women, Volume II.*, Valley Forge, Pennsylvania: Judson Press, 1988.

_____, *Women: To Preach Or Not To Preach*, Valley Forge, Pennsylvania: Judson Press, 1991.

Mitchell, Henry, *Black Preaching*, New York: Harper & Row, 1979.

_____, *Black Preaching: The Recovery Of A Powerful Art*, Nashville, Tennessee: Abingdon Press, 1990.

Myers, William H., *God's Yes Was Louder Than My No, Rethinking The African American Call To Ministry*, Grand Rapids, Michigan: Wm. B. Eerdmans Publishers, 1994.

_____, *The Irresistible Urge To Preach: A Collection Of Call Stories,* Grand Rapids, Michigan: Wm. B. Eerdmans Publishers.

Nee, Watchman, *The Ministry Of God's Word,* New York: Christian Fellowship Publishers, 1971.

Noren, Carol M., *The Woman In The Pulpit,* Nashville, Tennessee: Abingdon Press, 1992.

Ray, Sandy F., *Journeying Through A Jungle,* Nashville, Tennessee: Broadman Press, 1979.

Scott, Manuel, *Preacher Wait Your Turn,* Los Angeles, California: Manuel Scott Ministries.

Smith, J. Alfred, *Preach On,* Nashville, Tennessee: Broadman Press, 1984.

Stewart, Sr., Warren H., *Interpreting God's Word In Black Preaching,* Valley Forge, Pennsylvania: Judson Press, 1984.

Taylor, Gardner C., *How Shall They Preach,* Elgin, Illinois: Progressive Baptist Publishing House, 1977.

William & Johnson, Watley, Suzan D., *Preaching In Two Voices,* Valley Forge, Pennsylvania: Judson Press, 1992.

Wiedman, Judith, *Women Ministers, How Women Are Redefining Traditional Roles,* San Francisco, California: Harper and Row Publishers, 1973.

Warren and Wiersbe, Wiersbe, David *The Elements Of Preaching,* Wheaton, Illinois: Tyndale House, 1986.

Young, Henry J., *Preaching The Gospel,* Philadelphia, Pennsylvania: Fortress Press, 1976.

Endnotes

Preface

1   Leontyne Kelly, Fuller Theological Seminary Seminar, Pasadena, California, 1989, p. xi.

Introduction

2   William Augustus Jones, Jr., *Responsible Preaching*, (New Jersey: Aaron Press, 1989) p. 41.

3   This material is taken from *My Utmost for His Highest* by Oswald Chambers. Copyright (c) 1935 by Dodd Mead & Co., renewed (c) 1963 by the Oswald Chambers Publications Assn. Ltd., and is used by permission of Discovery House Publishers, Box 3566, Grand Rapids MI 49501. All rights reserved, p. 130

4   William H. Myers, *God's Yes Was Louder Than My No (Rethinking the African American Call to Ministry)*, (Michigan: Wm. B. Eerdmans Publishing Co., 1994) p. 234.

5   Brian Lanker, *I Have A Dream*, (NY: Stewart, Tabori & Chang, Inc., 1989) p. 112.

6   Fannie McDowell Hunter, *Women Preachers*, (Kentucky: Berachah Printing Co., 1905) p. 87-88.

7   William H. Myers, *Ibid.*, p. 28

8   9 Aimee Semple McPherson, *The Story of My Life*, (Waco, Texas: Word Books, 1973) p. 75.

9   Victoria Booth Demarest, *Sex & Spirit: God, Woman & Ministry*, (Florida: Valknrie Press, Inc., 1977) p. 155.

10 Victoria Booth Demarest, *Ibid.*, p. 158.

11 Jamie Buckingham, *Daughter of Destiny, Kathryn Kuhlman...Her Story*, Gwent, U.K. Valley Books, 1976) p. 46-47.

12 D. E. King, *Preaching To Preachers*, (Pennsylvania: Neibauer Press, 1984), p. 88.

13 D. E. King, *Preaching To Preachers*, (Pennsylvania: Neibauer Press, 1984), p. 89.

14 Hans Van Der Geest, *Presence in the Pulpit*, (Atlanta: John Knox Press, 1978) p. 144-145.

15 William Augustus Jones, Jr., *Ibid.*, p. 42-43

16 Dr. Ella Pearson Mitchell, *Those Preaching Women, Vol. I.*, Valley Forge: Judson Press, 1985) p. 13.

17 D. E. King, *Ibid.*, p. 91.

Chapter 1

18 W. E. Vine, *Expository Dictionary of New Testament Words*, (Minnesota: Minnesota, 1984), p. 894.

19 Dr. Warren H. Stewart, Sr., *If She's Alright With God Sermon*, at First Baptist Church, Redlands, October 9, 1994.

20 Fannie McDowell Hunter, *Ibid.*, p. 39.

21 Fannie McDowell Hunter, *Ibid.*, p. 37.

22 William H. Myers, *Ibid.*, p. 231

23 David A. Seamands, *Healing for Damaged Emotions*, (Chariot Victor Books, 1991) p. 20-23. Used by permission of Chariot Victor Publishing.

24 John & Paula Sandford, *Healing the Wounded Spirit*, (Oklahoma: Victory House, Inc., 1985) p. 59.

25 John & Paula Sandford, *Ibid.*, p. 5

26 Dr. James Henry, Ordination Service at First Baptist Church of Redlands, October 9, 1994.

27 Fannie McDowell Hunter, *Ibid.*, p. 91.

28 Beverly "Bam" Crawford, Beverly Crawford Ministries, Private collection tape series – *Women in Ministry - Free From Fear* – Tape 1, (Los Angeles, California: Crawford Ministries, 1987.

29 Fannie McDowell Hunter, *Ibid.*, p. 39.

30 Fushia Pickett, *God's Dream - His Eternal Plan For You*, (Pennsylvania: Destiny Image Publishers, 1991) p. 99.

31 Dr. Warren H. Stewart, Sr., *If She's Alright With God Sermon*, at First Baptist Church, Redlands, October 9, 1994.

32 Fannie McDowell Hunter, *Ibid.*, p. 99-100.

Chapter 2

33 William H. Myers, *Ibid.*, p. 145

34 William H. Myers, *Ibid.*, p. 238

35 W. K. Jackson, *I Let the Lord Do It – 65 Years in the Gospel Ministry*, (Oklahoma City: Campbell Road Press, 1994), p. 3.

36 William H. Myers, *Ibid.*, p. 135

37 Mike Murdock, *The Assignment* (Teaching Tapes), Eagle's Nest Church, Phoenix, Arizona 1992

Chapter 3

38 John Bevere, *Victory in the Wilderness*, (Apopka, Florida: John P. Bevere Ministries, 1192), p. 2.

39 Sandy F. Ray, *Journeying Through a Jungle*, (Tennessee: Broadman Press, 1979), p. 28-29.

40 Judith L. Wiedman, *Women Ministers, How Women Are*

Redefining Traditional Roles, San Francisco: Harper & Row Publishers, 1973) p. 94.

41   T. D. Jakes, *Water in the Wilderness*, (West Virginia: Pneuma Life Publishing, 1994), p. 14.

42   T. D. Jakes, *Ibid.*, p. 15.

43   Kim Clement, (Tape #5), Living Faith Christian Center, Northridge, California, July 9, 1995.

Chapter 4

44   William H. Myers, p. 130

Chapter 5

45   Judith L. Wiedman, *Ibid.*, p. 181.

46   Victoria Booth Demarest, *Ibid.*, p. 94.

Chapter 6

47   Ella Pearson Mitchell, *Women: To Preach or Not to Preach*, (21 Outstanding Black Preachers Say Yes!), (Pennsylvania: Judson Press, 1991) p. 17.

48   Victoria Booth Demarest, *Ibid.*, p. 94.

49   Charisma Magazine, November 1994, p. 26.

50   Ella Pearson Mitchell, *Ibid.*, Volume 2., p. 15

51   Ebony Magazine, November 1991, p. 106.

52   Judith L. Wiedman, *Ibid.*, p. 18.

53   William Augustus Jones, Jr., *Ibid.*, p. 41.

54   Anthony W. Green, Sermon, Second Baptist Church of Redlands, California, 1994.

Chapter 8

55   Gardner C. Taylor, *How Shall They Preach?*, (Illinois: Progressive Baptist Convention Publishing House, 1977), p. 59.

56 H. Beecher Hicks, *Correspondence with a Cripple from Tarsus (Romans in Dialogue with the 20th Century)*, (Michigan: Zondervan Publishing House, 1990), p. 33.

Acknowledgements

I want to thank the "midwives" that God sent into my life to help me birth my ministry to this point. Such "markers" as Pastor Beverly "Bam" Crawford, Dr. Alicia Broadous-Duncan, the Rev. Catherine Hughes, the Rev. M. Cecilia Broadus, the Rev. Jean Burch, the late Rev. Barbara Wilson, Dr. Minnie Clairborne, Sister Helen Harris, Sister B. J. Jenkins, Professor Julie Gorman, the Rev. Cindy Jacobs, Co-Pastor Bea Simms, Prophetess Cathy Fontenot, a dear friend, Jean Zeller who shared many of my dreams, and two faithful prayer warriors, Carrie Isaac and Allison Haynes. To an anointed artist, Denise Schnur, whom God knitted us together for the Kingdom's sake, I am thankful. I attribute the covers for several of my books to her artistic gift. To Vickie Stephens, I say a special thank you for the draft typing of this book. Vickie has been an "angel" in assisting me with many projects. And to Leslie Thomas for the initial formatting of the manuscript. He was a direct answer to prayer. Special thanks to Lillian Broadous and the Rev. Charlotte Hillman as proofreaders. Thanks also to Sandi Richey, my own personal librarian who helped me with much research.

Among markers that were men or couples, my husband,

Pastor Anthony W. Green, heads the list; then I must acknowledge my late grandparents, the Rev. and Mrs. H. B. Matthews, my late father-in-law, Pastor Frank Green, Dr. Warren H. Stewart, Sr., Pastor Reginald LeFall, the Rev. Glen Robertson, Bishop C. E. Simmons, Dr. Joe DeRoulhac, Bishop James Henry, Pastors Roy and Carolyn Harris, Pastor W. K. Jackson, and my brother-in-law, Les Wells, a faithful layman and spiritual confidant.

I thank God for my parents, Deacon Herbert and Lois Jackson, who remain a significant marker in my life.

For my children, I am most grateful to Elyzabeth, Kevin, Joel, Joseph and Joshua for sustaining all the changes Mommie had to go through in The Wilderness. I shall never forget my daughter Elyzabeth's comments when I was ordained: "Mom, you did it!"

Thanks to Keith Carroll of Destiny Image Publishers for his assistance in the early manuscript development.

And if it had not been for our pastorate at the Second Baptist Church of Redlands, California, this book would not have been birthed. I will always love them.

Special thanks to Ralph Tanner for his many years of expertise and wisdom in the publishing of the book, and Sue Diesness for her editorial advisement. Many hours have been given to birth this work.

God be praised for all the intercessors that stood with me with much prayer, service, sacrifice and love to see this project birthed. I am especially grateful to the staff of Jackie Green Ministries for their fasting and prayers, and for the "Friday Breakfast Table" Intercessors at the home of Cynthia Woods weekly.

My hope is that this book will be a "marker" for women preachers especially in The Wilderness of their calling. There are thirty thousand ordained women today according to Fuller Theological Seminary's March 1995 issue of Theology, News, & Notes featuring Women and Ministry. I believe there are twice as many women waiting for someone to help them birth their ministry.

To God be the glory for the great things He has done and will do through this book! It's His book for His Glory and because He's the Author and Finisher of our faith, I am confident that *When She Hears The Call* will bring healing, deliverance and reconciliation to His Body!

As He Orders My Steps,
Jackie L. Green

List of Contributors and Investors

Special thanks to the contributors and investors that were seed planters into this publication. *Denotes investors

Sarah Alexander
Marjorie Bennett
The Rev. Tina Buchanan
Elnora Brackins
The Rev. Sarahlyn Bristow
* Bill and Wylene Bridgeman
Gloria Broomfield
Shermaine Brown
Darlene Burkett
Doris Carrington
Dottie Cartwright
* Beverly Cave
Pastor Beverly "Bam"
Crawford, D.D.
Barbara Colbert
Willie Coppage
The Rev. Deborah Cotton
The Rev. Brenda Davis
Lateefa and Konata Doxey
* Judge Thomas Dunevant

Thelma Fagin
First Institutional Baptist
Church, Phoenix, AZ
Minister Cathy Fontenot
Thomas and Karen Frye
Mary Green
Mother Alice Greenwood
Jessie and Betty Hampton
* Allison Haynes
Dollie Heard
* Valerie Hollomon
* Honey Bears Restaurant
* Paul and Michele Hoskins
Monica Jackson
Mr. and Mrs. Kenneth Johnson
Julie Jolly
Bill and Juanita Kearney
Robin Kornegay
Stanley and Marjorie Kyle
Linda Lacy

Marva Lacy

Patricia Lee

* Dr. Vivian Little

* Kevin and Lavetta Meeks

The Rev. F. Lisa Miller

Lucretia Murphy

Pastor Joseph and Charlesetta Nixon

Kimberly Poore

Pastor Philip Powell

Eleanor Ragsdale

E. C. Reems Women's International, Arizona Chapter

Darian and Vickie Ross

The Rev. Brenda Rushing

* Mike and Denece Schnur

Kathy Shaw

The Rev. Jewel Harper Simon

Mother Marteal Singleton

Charmaine Woods

Linda Smith

* Mark and Anna Smith

The Rev. Yolanda Smith

Jesse Spencer

The Rev. Terry and Nicole Spencer

Thelma Staten

Dr. Eugene and Eva Stephens

The Rev. Tifphanie Rhymes

Irene Webb

Les Wells

Valerye Boyer-Wells

Wenonah Wells

* John and Flo Wilhight

Robert and Faye Williams

Annette Willis

Evangelist Birdie Willis

Lorraine Wilson

* Ron and Cynthia Woods

Everette and Loria Woods